Child Welfare Legal Representation

ABA Attorney Standards

AMERICAN BAR ASSOCIATION
Center on
Children and the Law
Access to Justice for Children & Families

Cover design by Lachina

Printed in the United States of America.

22 21 20 19 18   5 4 3 2 1

Library of Congress Cataloging-in-Publication Data
Names: ABA Center on Children and the Law.
Title: Child welfare legal representation : ABA attorney standards / edited by
    ABA Center on Children and the Law, American Bar Association.
Description: First edition. | Chicago : American Bar Association, 2018.
Identifiers: LCCN 2018031907 | ISBN 9781641052665 (print)
Subjects: LCSH: Child abuse—Law and legislation—United States. | Abused
    children—Legal status, laws, etc.—United States. | Parent and child
    (Law)—United States. | Legal assistance to children—United States.
Classification: LCC KF9323 .C59 2018 | DDC 344.7303/27—dc23
LC record available at https://lccn.loc.gov/2018031907

www.ShopABA.org

Contents

Legal Representation in Child Welfare Proceedings (Infographic)   148

Introduction

Over the last 50 years, there have been many changes in law and policy in the child welfare system. One constant, however, is the importance of high-quality legal representation. It is a constant that applies for parents, children, and the child welfare agency, all of whom play critical roles in judicial proceedings that determine the composition of individual families and relationships under the law.

One reason legal representation is important in such cases arises from the high stakes involved. For example, for children these cases involve rights that concern family, kin, school, medical care, and personal safety. For parents, these cases involve the right to parent one's child as well as important rights to privacy and freedom from government interference. And for the child welfare agency, representation is key because agencies have the daunting task of serving society's interest in keeping children safe while simultaneously protecting family integrity.

In addition to protecting individual rights and representing governmental interests, research shows high-quality legal representation serves another critical role: improving the effectiveness of the system as a whole. For example, children represented by counsel have a significantly higher rate of exit to permanency than children not represented by counsel.[1] Other studies on child representation have established that early appointment of counsel in a child's case can directly impact rates of exit to permanency within the first six months of a case.[2] Similarly, studies of parent representation show that when parents are represented by an interdisciplinary team (as supported by the ABA standards) their children's exit rate to reunification, adoption and guardianship is significantly higher and the time to these permanency outcomes is shorter.[3]

This makes sense. When parties have an attorney advocating for them it increases their overall participation in the case, which in turn leads to more tailored case plans, improved perceptions of fairness, and a more informed, better judicial decision-making process.

In light of the expanding understanding that attorney participation protects legal rights and interests in a case, and improves the system's functioning, these ABA attorney standards have never been more important. When originally developed in 1996, 2004, and 2006 respectively, each set of standards was written with two goals: to recognize and help attorneys navigate the challenges of day-to-day practice in child welfare law, and to raise the quality of child welfare legal representation as much as possible.

A third use we seek to facilitate by printing all three representation standards and the Model Act together in this book is encouraging attorneys to understand each other's roles in the system. In other words, if you are a children's attorney, we recommend you review the standards that apply to your daily work but also that you read those standards that apply to your colleagues who represent parents and agencies. The same is recommended for attorneys who represent parents and agencies.

When considering the ways this system differs from traditional American legal structures, there is perhaps no legal system more complex than child welfare. For example, child welfare law involves three parties rather than the two-party structure of most of American criminal and civil law. Adding to the complexity is the fact that judges must look not only retroactively at whether an action did or did not happen, they must examine how things are happening in real time and prospectively evaluate the likelihood of other actions occurring in the future, a far-cry from typical judicial roles of applying law to facts. Finally, although the child welfare legal system is largely adversarial, the principles underlying it seek to facilitate shared goals such as reunification and children's best interests, which all three parties seek to achieve though different means.

In light of these layers of complexity, one critical aspect of representation in this system involves understanding not only one's role within it, but also how that role is shaped by and interfaces with the other parties and other counsel involved. We hope that by combining these attorney representation standards we can support your daily practice, strengthen the quality of your representation for your clients, and help you understand what those goals may be for the other attorneys on the case.

Finally, I want to take a moment to thank you. Thank you for entering this important legal field, for the ongoing work you do to seek access to justice for children and families under the law, and for relying on the ABA Center on Children and the Law to support your professional growth and development. You are the reason these standards were developed over the last 25 years and you are the reason we want to make them even more accessible in this book.

Prudence Beidler Carr
ABA Center on Children and the Law, Director

NOTES

1. Zinn A.E. & J. Slowriver. *Expediting Permanency: Legal Representation for Foster Children in Palm Beach County.* Chicago: Chapin Hall Center for Children at the University of Chicago, 2008.
2. Orlebeke, B., X. Zhou, A. Skyles & A. Zinn. *Evaluation of the QIC-ChildRep Best Practice Model Training for Attorneys Representing Children in Child Welfare.* Chicago: Chapin Hall Center for Children at the University of Chicago, 2016.
3. Courtney, M., J. Hook & M. Orme. *Evaluation of the Impact of Enhanced Parental Legal Representation on the Timing of Permanency Outcomes for Children in Foster Care.* Partners for Our Children at the University of Washington, 2011.

Standards of Practice for Lawyers Who Represent Children in Abuse and Neglect Cases

FEBRUARY 1996

PREFACE

All children subject to court proceedings involving allegations of child abuse and neglect should have legal representation as long as the court jurisdiction continues. These Abuse and Neglect Standards are meant to apply when a lawyer is appointed for a child in any legal action based on: (a) a petition filed for protection of the child; (b) a request to a court to change legal custody, visitation, or guardianship based on allegations of child abuse or neglect based on sufficient cause; or (c) an action to terminate parental rights.

These standards apply only to lawyers and take the position that although a lawyer *may* accept appointment in the dual capacity of a "lawyer/guardian ad litem," the lawyer's primary duty must still be focused on the protection of the legal rights of the child client. The lawyer/guardian ad litem should therefore perform all the functions of a "child's attorney," except as otherwise noted.

These standards build upon the ABA-approved *Juvenile Justice Standards Relating to Counsel for Private Parties* (1979) which include important directions for lawyers representing children in juvenile court matters generally, but do not contain sufficient guidance to aid lawyers representing children in abuse and neglect cases. These Abuse and Neglect Standards are also intended to help implement a series of

ABA-approved policy resolutions (in Appendix) on the importance of legal representation and the improvement of lawyer practice in child protection cases.

In support of having lawyers play an active role in child abuse and neglect cases, in August 1995 the ABA endorsed a set of *Resource Guidelines: Improving Court Practice in Child Abuse & Neglect Cases* produced by the National Council of Juvenile and Family Court Judges. The *Resource Guidelines* stress the importance of quality representation provided by competent and diligent lawyers by supporting: 1) the approach of vigorous representation of child clients; and 2) the actions that courts should take to help assure such representation.

These standards contain two parts. Part I addresses the specific roles and responsibilities of a lawyer appointed to represent a child in an abuse and neglect case. Part II provides a set of standards for judicial administrators and trial judges to assure high quality legal representation.

PART 1: STANDARDS FOR THE CHILD'S ATTORNEY

A. Definitions

A-1. The Child's Attorney. The term "child's attorney" means a lawyer who provides legal services for a child and who owes the same duties of undivided loyalty, confidentiality, and competent representation to the child as is due an adult client.

Commentary
These standards explicitly recognize that the child is a separate individual with potentially discrete and independent views. To ensure that the child's independent voice is heard, the child's attorney must advocate the child's articulated position. Consequently, the child's attorney owes traditional duties to the child as client consistent with ER 1.14(a) of the Model Rules of Professional Conduct. In all but the exceptional case, such as with a preverbal child, the child's attorney will maintain this traditional relationship with the child/client. As with any client, the child's attorney may counsel against the pursuit of a particular position sought by the child. The child's attorney should recognize that the child may be more susceptible to intimidation and manipulation than some adult clients. Therefore, the child's attorney should ensure that the decision the child ultimately makes reflects his or her actual position.

A-2. Lawyer Appointed as Guardian Ad Litem. A lawyer appointed as "guardian ad litem" for a child is an officer of the court appointed to protect the child's interests without being bound by the child's expressed preferences.

Commentary

In some jurisdictions the lawyer may be appointed as guardian ad litem. These standards, however, express a clear preference for the appointment as the "child's attorney." These standards address the lawyer's obligations to the child as client.

A lawyer appointed as guardian ad litem is almost inevitably expected to perform legal functions on behalf of the child. Where the local law permits, the lawyer is expected to act in the dual role of guardian ad litem and lawyer of record. The chief distinguishing factor between the roles is the manner and method to be followed in determining the legal position to be advocated. While a guardian ad litem should take the child's point of view into account, the child's preferences are not binding, irrespective of the child's age and the ability or willingness of the child to express preferences. Moreover, in many states, a guardian ad litem may be required by statute or custom to perform specific tasks, such as submitting a report or testifying as a fact or expert witness. These tasks are not part of functioning as a "lawyer."

These standards do not apply to nonlawyers when such persons are appointed as guardians ad litem or as "court appointed special advocates" (CASA). The nonlawyer guardian ad litem cannot and should not be expected to perform any legal functions on behalf of a child.

A-3. Developmentally Appropriate. "Developmentally appropriate" means that the child's attorney should ensure the child's ability to provide client-based directions by structuring all communications to account for the individual child's age, level of education, cultural context, and degree of language acquisition.

Commentary

The lawyer has an obligation to explain clearly, precisely, and in terms the client can understand the meaning and consequences of action.[1] A child client may not understand the legal terminology and for a variety of reasons may choose a particular course of action without fully appreciating the implications. With a child the potential for not understanding may be even greater. Therefore, the child's attorney has additional obligations based on the child's age, level of education, and degree of language acquisition. There is also the possibility that because of a particular child's developmental limitations, the lawyer may not completely understand the child's responses. Therefore, the child's attorney must learn how to ask developmentally appropriate questions and how to interpret the child's responses.[2] The child's attorney may work with social workers or other professionals to assess a child's developmental abilities and to facilitate communication.

B. General Authority and Duties

B-1. Basic Obligations. The child's attorney should:

1. Obtain copies of all pleadings and relevant notices;
2. Participate in depositions, negotiations, discovery, pretrial conferences, and hearings;
3. Inform other parties and their representatives that he or she is representing the child and expects reasonable notification prior to case conferences, changes of placement, and other changes of circumstances affecting the child and the child's family;
4. Attempt to reduce case delays and ensure that the court recognizes the need to speedily promote permanency for the child;
5. Counsel the child concerning the subject matter of the litigation, the child's rights, the court system, the proceedings, the lawyer's role, and what to expect in the legal process;
6. Develop a theory and strategy of the case to implement at hearings, including factual and legal issues; and
7. Identify appropriate family and professional resources for the child.

Commentary
The child's attorney should not be merely a fact-finder, but rather, should zealously advocate a position on behalf of the child. (The same is true for the guardian ad litem, although the position to be advocated may be different). In furtherance of that advocacy, the child's attorney must be adequately prepared prior to hearings. The lawyer's presence at and active participation in all hearings is absolutely critical.[3]

Although the child's position may overlap with the position of one or both parents, third-party caretakers, or a state agency, the child's attorney should be prepared to participate fully in any proceedings and not merely defer to the other parties. Any identity of position should be based on the merits of the position, and not a mere endorsement of another party's position.

While subsection (4) recognizes that delays are usually harmful, there may be some circumstances when delay may be beneficial. Section (7) contemplates that the child's attorney will identify counseling, educational and health services, substance abuse programs for the child and other family members, housing and other forms of material assistance for which the child may qualify under law. The lawyer can also identify family members, friends, neighbors, or teachers with whom the child feels it is important to maintain contact; mentoring programs, such as Big Brother/Big Sister; recreational opportunities that develop social skills and self-esteem; educational support programs; and volunteer opportunities which can enhance a child's self-esteem.

B-2. Conflict Situations. (1) If a lawyer appointed as guardian ad litem determines that there is a conflict caused by performing both roles of guardian ad litem and child's attorney, the lawyer should continue to perform as the child's attorney and withdraw as guardian ad litem. The lawyer should request appointment of a guardian ad litem without revealing the basis for the request.

(2) If a lawyer is appointed as a "child's attorney" for siblings, there may also be a conflict which could require that the lawyer decline representation or withdraw from representing all of the children.

Commentary
The primary conflict that arises between the two roles is when the child's expressed preferences differ from what the lawyer deems to be in the child's best interests. As a practical matter, when the lawyer has established a trusting relationship with the child, most conflicts can be avoided. While the lawyer should be careful not to apply undue pressure to a child, the lawyer's advice and guidance can often persuade the child to change an imprudent position or to identify alternative choices if the child's first choice is denied by the court.

The lawyer-client role involves a confidential relationship with privileged communications, while a guardian ad litem-client role may not be confidential.[4] Because the child has a right to confidentiality and advocacy of his or her position, the child's attorney can never abandon this role. Once a lawyer has a lawyer-client relationship with a minor, he or she cannot and should not assume any other role for the child, especially as guardian ad litem. When the roles cannot be reconciled, another person must assume the guardian ad litem role.[5]

B-3. Client under Disability. The child's attorney should determine whether the child is "under a disability" pursuant to the Model Rules of Professional Conduct or the Model Code of Professional Responsibility with respect to each issue in which the child is called upon to direct the representation.

Commentary
These standards do not accept the idea that children of certain ages are "impaired," "disabled," "incompetent," or lack capacity to determine their position in litigation. Further, these standards reject the concept that any disability must be globally determined.

Rather, disability is contextual, incremental, and may be intermittent. The child's ability to contribute to a determination of his or her position is functional, depending upon the particular position and the circumstances prevailing at the time the position must be determined. Therefore, a child may be able to determine some positions in the case but not others. Similarly, a child may be able to direct the lawyer with respect to a particular issue at one time but not at another. This Standard relies on empirical knowledge about competencies with respect to both adults and children.[6]

B-4. Client Preferences. The child's attorney should elicit the child's preferences in a developmentally appropriate manner, advise the child, and provide guidance. The child's attorney should represent the child's expressed preferences and follow the child's direction throughout the course of litigation.

Commentary
The lawyer has a duty to explain to the child in a developmentally appropriate way such information as will assist the child in having maximum input in determination of the particular position at issue. The lawyer should inform the child of the relevant facts and applicable laws and the ramifications of taking various positions, which may include the impact of such decisions on other family members or on future legal proceedings. The lawyer may express an opinion concerning the likelihood of the court or other parties accepting particular positions. The lawyer may inform the child of an expert's recommendations germane to the issue.

As in any other lawyer/client relationship, the lawyer may express his or her assessment of the case, the best position for the child to take, and the reasons underlying such recommendation. A child, however, may agree with the lawyer for inappropriate reasons. A lawyer must remain aware of the power dynamics inherent in adult/child relationships. Therefore, the lawyer needs to understand what the child knows and what factors are influencing the child's decision. The lawyer should attempt to determine from the child's opinion and reasoning what factors have been most influential or have been confusing or glided over by the child when deciding the best time to express his or her assessment of the case.

Consistent with the rules of confidentiality and with sensitivity to the child's privacy, the lawyer should consult with the child's therapist and other experts and obtain appropriate records. For example, a child's therapist may help the child to understand why an expressed position is dangerous, foolish, or not in the child's best interests. The therapist might also assist the lawyer in understanding the child's perspective, priorities, and individual needs. Similarly, significant persons in the child's life may educate the lawyer about the child's needs, priorities, and previous experiences.

The lawyer for the child has dual fiduciary duties to the child which must be balanced. On one hand, the lawyer has a duty to ensure that the child client is given the information necessary to make an informed decision, including advice and guidance. On the other hand, the lawyer has a duty not to overbear the will of the child.

While the lawyer may attempt to persuade the child to accept a particular position, the lawyer may not advocate a position contrary to the child's expressed position except as provided by these Abuse and Neglect Standards or the Code of Professional Responsibility.

While the child is entitled to determine the overall objectives to be pursued, the child's attorney, as any adult's lawyer, may make certain decisions with respect to the manner of achieving those objectives, particularly with respect to procedural matters. These Abuse and Neglect standards do not require the lawyer to consult with the child on matters which would not require consultation with an adult client. Further, the standards do not require the child's attorney to discuss with the child issues for which it is not feasible to obtain the child's direction because of the child's developmental limitations, as with an infant or preverbal child.

1. **To the extent that a child cannot express a preference, the child's attorney shall make a good faith effort to determine the child's wishes and advocate accordingly or request appointment of a guardian ad litem.**

Commentary

There are circumstances in which a child is unable to express a position, as in the case of a preverbal child, or may not be capable of understanding the legal or factual issues involved. Under such circumstances, the child's attorney should continue to represent the child's legal interests and request appointment of a guardian ad litem. This limitation distinguishes the scope of independent decision-making of the child's attorney and a person acting as guardian ad litem.

2. **To the extent that a child does not or will not express a preference about particular issues, the child's attorney should determine and advocate the child's legal interests.**

Commentary

The child's failure to express a position is distinguishable from a directive that the lawyer not take a position with respect to certain issues. The child may have no opinion with respect to a particular issue, or may delegate the decision-making authority. For example, the child may not want to assume the responsibility of expressing a position because of loyalty conflicts or the desire not to hurt one of the other parties. The lawyer should clarify with the child whether the child wants the lawyer to take a position or remain silent with respect to that issue or wants the preference expressed only if the parent or other party is out of the courtroom. The lawyer is then bound by the child's directive. The position taken by the lawyer should not contradict or undermine other issues about which the child has expressed a preference.

3. **If the child's attorney determines that the child's expressed preference would be seriously injurious to the child (as opposed to merely being contrary to the lawyer's opinion of what would be in the child's interests), the lawyer may request appointment of a separate guardian ad litem and continue to represent the child's expressed preference, unless the child's position is prohibited by law or without any factual foundation. The child's attorney shall not reveal the basis of the request for appointment of a guardian ad litem which would compromise the child's position.**

Commentary

One of the most difficult ethical issues for lawyers representing children occurs when the child is able to express a position and does so, but the lawyer believes that the position chosen is wholly inappropriate or could result in serious injury to the child. This is particularly likely to happen with respect to an abused child whose home is unsafe, but who desires to remain or return home. A child may desire to live in a dangerous situation because it is all he or she knows, because of a feeling of blame or of responsibility to take care of the parents, or because of threats. The child may choose to deal with a known situation rather than risk the unknown world of a foster home or other out-of-home placement.

In most cases the ethical conflict involved in asserting a position which would seriously endanger the child, especially by disclosure of privileged information, can be resolved through the lawyer's counseling function. If the lawyer has taken the time to establish rapport with the child and gain that child's trust, it is likely that the lawyer will be able to persuade the child to abandon a dangerous position or at least identify an alternate course.

If the child cannot be persuaded, the lawyer has a duty to safeguard the child's interests by requesting appointment of a guardian ad litem, who will be charged with advocating the child's best interests without being bound by the child's direction. As a practical matter, this may not adequately protect the child if the danger to the child was revealed only in a confidential disclosure to the lawyer, because the guardian ad litem may never learn of the disclosed danger.

Confidentiality is abrogated for various professionals by mandatory child abuse reporting laws. Some states abrogate lawyer-client privilege by mandating reports. States which do not abrogate the privilege may permit reports notwithstanding professional privileges. The policy considerations underlying abrogation apply to lawyers where there is a substantial danger of serious injury or death. Under such circumstances, the lawyer must take the minimum steps which would be necessary to ensure the child's safety, respecting and following the child's direction to the greatest extent possible consistent with the child's safety and ethical rules.

The lawyer may never counsel a client or assist a client in conduct the lawyer knows is criminal or fraudulent.[7] Further, existing ethical rules require the lawyer to disclose confidential information to the extent necessary to prevent the client from committing a criminal act likely to result in death or substantial bodily harm,[8] and permits the lawyer to reveal the intention of the client to commit a crime.[9] While child abuse, including sexual abuse, are crimes, the child is presumably the victim, rather than the perpetrator of those crimes. Therefore, disclosure of confidences is designed to protect the client, rather than to protect a third party from the client. Where the child is in grave danger of serious injury or death, the child's safety must be the paramount concern.

The lawyer is not bound to pursue the client's objectives through means not permitted by law and ethical rules.[10] Further, lawyers may be subject personally to sanctions for taking positions that are not well grounded in fact and warranted by existing law or a good faith argument for the extension, modification, or reversal of existing law.

B-5. Child's Interests. The determination of the child's legal interests should be based on objective criteria as set forth in the law that are related to the purposes of the proceedings. The criteria should address the child's specific needs and preferences, the goal of expeditious resolution of the case so the child can remain or return home or be placed in a safe, nurturing, and permanent environment, and the use of the least restrictive or detrimental alternatives available.

Commentary
A lawyer who is required to determine the child's interests is functioning in a nontraditional role by determining the position to be advocated independently of the client. The lawyer should base the position, however, on objective criteria concerning the child's needs and interests, and not merely on the lawyer's personal values, philosophies, and experiences. The child's various needs and interests may be in conflict and must be weighed against each other. Even nonverbal children can communicate their needs and interests through their behaviors and developmental levels.[11] The lawyer may seek the advice and consultation of experts and other knowledgeable people in both determining and weighing such needs and interests.

A child's legal interests may include basic physical and emotional needs, such as safety, shelter, food, and clothing. Such needs should be assessed in light of the child's vulnerability, dependence upon others, available external resources, and the degree of risk. A child needs family affiliation and stability of placement. The child's developmental level, including his or her sense of time, is relevant to an assessment of need. For example, a very young child may be less able to tolerate separation from a primary caretaker than an older child, and if separation is necessary, more frequent visitation than is ordinarily provided may be necessary.

In general, a child prefers to live with known people, to continue normal activities, and to avoid moving. To that end, the child's attorney should determine whether relatives, friends, neighbors, or other people known to the child are appropriate and available as placement resources. The lawyer must determine the child's feelings about the proposed caretaker, however, because familiarity does not automatically confer positive regard. Further, the lawyer may need to balance competing stability interests, such as living with a relative in another town versus living in a foster home in the same neighborhood. The individual child's needs will influence this balancing task.

In general, a child needs decisions about the custodial environment to be made quickly. Therefore, if the child must be removed from the home, it is generally in the child's best interests to have rehabilitative or reunification services offered to the family quickly. On the other hand, if it appears that reunification will be unlikely, it is generally in the child's best interests to move quickly toward an alternative permanent plan. Delay and indecision are rarely in a child's best interests.

In addition to the general needs and interests of children, individual children have particular needs, and the lawyer must determine the child client's individual needs. There are few rules which apply across the board to all children under all circumstances.

C. Actions to Be Taken

C-1. Meet with Child. Establishing and maintaining a relationship with a child is the foundation of representation. Therefore, irrespective of the child's age, the child's attorney should visit with the child prior to court hearings and when apprised of emergencies or significant events impacting on the child.

Commentary
Meeting with the child is important before court hearings and case reviews. In addition, changes in placement, school suspensions, inpatient hospitalizations, and other similar changes warrant meeting again with the child. Such in-person meetings allow the lawyer to explain to the child what is happening, what alternatives might be available, and what will happen next. This also allows the lawyer to assess the child's circumstances, often leading to a greater understanding of the case, which may lead to more creative solutions in the child's interest. A lawyer can learn a great deal from meeting with child clients, including a preverbal child.[12]

C-2. Investigate. To support the client's position, the child's attorney should conduct thorough, continuing, and independent investigations and discovery which may include, but should not be limited to:

1. **Reviewing the child's social services, psychiatric, psychological, drug and alcohol, medical, law enforcement, school, and other records relevant to the case;**

Commentary
Thorough, independent investigation of cases, at every stage of the proceedings, is a key aspect of providing competent representation to children.[13] The lawyer may need to use subpoenas or other discovery or motion procedures to obtain the relevant records, especially those records which pertain to the other parties. In some jurisdictions the statute or the order appointing the lawyer for the child includes provision for obtaining certain records.

2. **Reviewing the court files of the child and siblings, case-related records of the social service agency and other service providers;**

Commentary
Another key aspect of representing children is the review of all documents submitted to the court as well as relevant agency case files and law enforcement reports.[14] Other relevant files that should be reviewed include those concerning child protective services, developmental disabilities, juvenile delinquency, mental health, and educational agencies. These records can provide a more complete context for the current problems of the child and family. Information in the files may suggest additional professionals and lay witnesses who should be contacted and may reveal alternate potential placements and services.

3. **Contacting lawyers for other parties and nonlawyer guardians ad litem or court-appointed special advocates (CASA) for background information;**

Commentary
The other parties' lawyers may have information not included in any of the available records. Further, they can provide information on their respective clients' perspectives. The CASA is typically charged with performing an independent factual investigation, getting to know the child, and speaking up to the court on the child's "best interests." Volunteer CASAs may have more time to perform their functions than the child's attorney and can often provide a great deal of information to assist the child's attorney. Where there appears to be role conflict or confusion over the involvement of both a child's attorney and CASA in the same case, there should be joint efforts to clarify and define mutual responsibilities.[15]

4. Contacting and meeting with the parents/legal guardians/caretakers of the child, with permission of their lawyer;

Commentary

Such contact generally should include visiting the home, which will give the lawyer additional information about the child's custodial circumstances.

5. Obtaining necessary authorizations for the release of information;

Commentary

If the relevant statute or order appointing the lawyer for the child does not provide explicit authorization for the lawyer's obtaining necessary records, the lawyer should attempt to obtain authorizations for release of information from the agency and from the parents, with their lawyer's consent. Even if it is not required, an older child should be asked to sign authorizations for release of his or her own records, because such a request demonstrates the lawyer's respect for the client's authority over information.

6. Interviewing individuals involved with the child, including school personnel, child welfare caseworkers, foster parents and other caretakers, neighbors, relatives, school personnel, coaches, clergy, mental health professionals, physicians, law enforcement officers, and other potential witnesses;

Commentary

In some jurisdictions the child's attorney is permitted free access to agency caseworkers. In others, contact with the caseworker must be arranged through the agency's lawyer.

7. Reviewing relevant photographs, video or audio tapes and other evidence; and

Commentary

It is essential that the lawyer review the evidence personally, rather than relying on other parties' or counsel's descriptions and characterizations of the evidence.

8. Attending treatment, placement, administrative hearings, other proceedings involving legal issues, and school case conferences or staffings concerning the child as needed.

Commentary

While some courts will not authorize compensation for the child's attorney to attend such collateral meetings, such attendance is often very important. The child's attorney can present the child's perspective at such meetings, as well as gather information necessary to proper representation. In some cases the child's attorney can be pivotal in achieving a negotiated settlement of all or some issues. The child's attorney may not need to attend collateral meetings if another person involved in the case, such as a social worker who works with the lawyer, can get the information or present the child's perspective.

C-3. File Pleadings. The child's attorney should file petitions, motions, responses or objections as necessary to represent the child. Relief requested may include, but is not limited to:

1. A mental or physical examination of a party or the child;
2. A parenting, custody or visitation evaluation;
3. An increase, decrease, or termination of contact or visitation;
4. Restraining or enjoining a change of placement;
5. Contempt for noncompliance with a court order;
6. Termination of the parent-child relationship;
7. Child support;
8. A protective order concerning the child's privileged communications or tangible or intangible property;
9. Request services for child or family; and
10. Dismissal of petitions or motions.

Commentary

Filing and arguing necessary motions is an essential part of the role of a child's attorney.[16] Unless the lawyer is serving in a role which explicitly precludes the filing of pleadings, the lawyer should file any appropriate pleadings on behalf of the child, including responses to the pleadings of the other parties. The filing of such pleadings can ensure that appropriate issues are properly before the court and can expedite the court's consideration of issues important to the child's interests. In some jurisdictions, guardians ad litem are not permitted to file pleadings, in which case it should be clear to the lawyer that he or she is not the "child's attorney" as defined in these standards.

C-4. Request Services. Consistent with the child's wishes, the child's attorney should seek appropriate services (by court order if necessary) to access entitlements, to protect the child's interests and to implement a service plan. These services may include, but not be limited to:

1. Family preservation-related prevention or reunification services;
2. Sibling and family visitation;
3. Child support;
4. Domestic violence prevention, intervention, and treatment;
5. Medical and mental health care;
6. Drug and alcohol treatment;
7. Parenting education;
8. Semi-independent and independent living services;
9. Long-term foster care;
10. Termination of parental rights action;
11. Adoption services;
12. Education;
13. Recreational or social services; and
14. Housing.

Commentary
The lawyer should request appropriate services even if there is no hearing scheduled. Such requests may be made to the agency or treatment providers, or if such informal methods are unsuccessful, the lawyer should file a motion to bring the matter before the court. In some cases the child's attorney should file collateral actions, such as petitions for termination of parental rights, if such an action would advance the child's interest and is legally permitted and justified. Different resources are available in different localities.

C-5. Child with Special Needs. Consistent with the child's wishes, the child's attorney should assure that a child with special needs receives appropriate services to address the physical, mental, or developmental disabilities.

These services may include, but should not be limited to:

1. Special education and related services;
2. Supplemental security income (SSI) to help support needed services;
3. Therapeutic foster or group home care; and
4. Residential/in-patient and out-patient psychiatric treatment.

Commentary
There are many services available from extra-judicial, as well as judicial, sources for children with special needs. The child's attorney should be familiar with these other services and how to assure their availability for the client.[17]

C-6. Negotiate Settlements. The child's attorney should participate in settlement negotiations to seek expeditious resolution of the case, keeping in mind the effect of continuances and delays on the child. The child's attorney should use suitable mediation resources.

Commentary
Particularly in contentious cases, the child's attorney may effectively assist negotiations of the parties and their lawyers by focusing on the needs of the child. If a parent is legally represented, it is unethical for the child's attorney to negotiate with a parent directly without the consent of the parent's lawyer. Because the court is likely to resolve at least some parts of the dispute in question based on the best interests of the child, the child's attorney is in a pivotal position in negotiation.

Settlement frequently obtains at least short-term relief for all parties involved and is often the best resolution of a case. The child's attorney, however, should not become merely a facilitator to the parties' reaching a negotiated settlement. As developmentally appropriate, the child's attorney should consult the child prior to any settlement becoming binding.

D. Hearings

D-1. Court Appearances. The child's attorney should attend all hearings and participate in all telephone or other conferences with the court unless a particular hearing involves issues completely unrelated to the child.

D-2. Client Explanation. The child's attorney should explain to the client, in a developmentally appropriate manner, what is expected to happen before, during and after each hearing.

D-3. Motions and Objections. The child's attorney should make appropriate motions, including motions *in limine* and evidentiary objections, to advance the child's position at trial or during other hearings. If necessary, the child's attorney should file briefs in support of evidentiary issues. Further, during all hearings, the child's attorney should preserve legal issues for appeal, as appropriate.

D-4. Presentation of Evidence. The child's attorney should present and cross examine witnesses, offer exhibits, and provide independent evidence as necessary.

Commentary

The child's position may overlap with the positions of one or both parents, third-party caretakers, or a child protection agency. Nevertheless, the child's attorney should be prepared to participate fully in every hearing and not merely defer to the other parties. Any identity of position should be based on the merits of the position (consistent with Standard B-6), and not a mere endorsement of another party's position.

D-5. Child at Hearing. In most circumstances, the child should be present at significant court hearings, regardless of whether the child will testify.

Commentary

A child has the right to meaningful participation in the case, which generally includes the child's presence at significant court hearings. Further, the child's presence underscores for the judge that the child is a real party in interest in the case. It may be necessary to obtain a court order or writ of habeas corpus ad testificandum to secure the child's attendance at the hearing.

A decision to exclude the child from the hearing should be made based on a particularized determination that the child does not want to attend, is too young to sit through the hearing, would be severely traumatized by such attendance, or for other good reason would be better served by nonattendance. There may be other extraordinary reasons for the child's non-attendance. The lawyer should consult the child, therapist, caretaker, or any other knowledgeable person in determining the effect on the child of being present at the hearing. In some jurisdictions the court requires an affirmative waiver of the child's presence if the child will not attend. Even a child who is too young to sit through the hearing may benefit from seeing the courtroom and meeting, or at least seeing, the judge who will be making the decisions. The lawyer should provide the court with any required notice that the child will be present. Concerns about the child being exposed to certain parts of the evidence may be addressed by the child's temporary exclusion from the courtroom during the taking of that evidence, rather than by excluding the child from the entire hearing.

The lawyer should ensure that the state/custodian meets its obligation to transport the child to and from the hearing. Similarly, the lawyer should ensure the presence of someone to accompany the child any time the child is temporarily absent from the hearing.

D-6. Whether Child Should Testify. The child's attorney should decide whether to call the child as a witness. The decision should include consideration of the child's need or desire to testify, any repercussions of testifying, the necessity of the child's direct testimony, the availability of other evidence or hearsay exceptions which may substitute for direct testimony by the child, and the child's developmental ability to provide direct testimony and withstand possible cross-examination. Ultimately, the child's attorney is bound by the child's direction concerning testifying.

Commentary

There are no blanket rules regarding a child's testimony. While testifying is undoubtedly traumatic for many children, it is therapeutic and empowering for others. Therefore, the decision about the child's testifying should be made individually, based on the circumstances of the individual child and the individual case. The child's therapist, if any, should be consulted both with respect to the decision itself and assistance with preparation. In the absence of compelling reasons, a child who has a strong desire to testify should be called to do so.[18] If the child should not wish to testify or would be harmed by being forced to testify, the lawyer should seek a stipulation of the parties not to call the child as a witness or seek a protective order from the court. If the child is compelled to testify, the lawyer should seek to minimize the adverse consequences by seeking any appropriate accommodations permitted by local law, such as having the testimony taken informally, in chambers, without presence of the parents.[19] The child should know whether the in-chambers testimony will be shared with others, such as parents who might be excluded from chambers, before agreeing to this forum. The lawyer should also prepare the child for the possibility that the judge may render a decision against the child's wishes which will not be the child's fault.

D-7. Child Witness. The child's attorney should prepare the child to testify. This should include familiarizing the child with the courtroom, court procedures, and what to expect during direct and cross-examination and ensuring that testifying will cause minimum harm to the child.

Commentary

The lawyer's preparation of the child to testify should include attention to the child's developmental needs and abilities as well as to accommodations which should be made by the court and other lawyers. The lawyer should seek any necessary assistance from the court, including location of the testimony (in chambers, at a small table etc.), determination of who will be present, and restrictions on the manner and phrasing of questions posed to the child.

The accuracy of children's testimony is enhanced when they feel comfortable.[20] Courts have permitted support persons to be present in the courtroom, sometimes even with the child sitting on the person's lap to testify. Because child abuse and neglect cases are often closed to the public, special permission may be necessary to enable such persons to be present during hearings. Further, where the rule sequestering witnesses has been invoked, the order of witnesses may need to be changed or an exemption granted where the support person also will be a witness. The child should be asked whether he or she would like someone to be present, and if so, whom the child prefers. Typical support persons include parents, relatives, therapists, Court Appointed Special Advocates (CASA), social workers, victim-witness advocates, and members of the clergy. For some, presence of the child's attorney provides sufficient support.

D-8. Questioning the Child. The child's attorney should seek to ensure that questions to the child are phrased in a syntactically and linguistically appropriate manner.

Commentary
The phrasing of questions should take into consideration the law and research regarding children's testimony, memory, and suggestibility.[21]

The information a child gives in interviews and during testimony is often misleading because the adults have not understood how to ask children developmentally appropriate questions and how to interpret their answers properly.[22] The child's attorney must become skilled at recognizing the child's developmental limitations. It may be appropriate to present expert testimony on the issue and even to have an expert present during a young child's testimony to point out any developmentally inappropriate phrasing.

D-9. Challenges to Child's Testimony/Statements. The child's competency to testify, or the reliability of the child's testimony or out-of-court statements, may be called into question. The child's attorney should be familiar with the current law and empirical knowledge about children's competency, memory, and suggestibility and, where appropriate, attempt to establish the competency and reliability of the child.

Commentary
Many jurisdictions have abolished presumptive ages of competency.[23] The jurisdictions which have rejected presumptive ages for testimonial competency have applied more flexible, case-by-case analyses.[24] Competency to testify involves the abilities to perceive and relate.

If necessary, the child's attorney should present expert testimony to establish competency or reliability or to rehabilitate any impeachment of the child on those bases.[25]

D-10. Jury Selection. In those states in which a jury trial is possible, the child's attorney should participate in jury selection and drafting jury instructions.

D-11. Conclusion of Hearing. If appropriate, the child's attorney should make a closing argument, and provide proposed findings of fact and conclusions of law. The child's attorney should ensure that a written order is entered.

Commentary
One of the values of having a trained child's attorney is such a lawyer can often present creative alternative solutions to the court. Further, the child's attorney is able to argue the child's interests from the child's perspective, keeping the case focused on the child's needs and the effect of various dispositions on the child.

D-12. Expanded Scope of Representation. The child's attorney may request authority from the court to pursue issues on behalf of the child, administratively or judicially, even if those issues do not specifically arise from the court appointment. For example:

1. Child support;
2. Delinquency or status offender matters;
3. SSI and other public benefits;
4. Custody;
5. Guardianship;
6. Paternity;
7. Personal injury;
8. School/education issues, especially for a child with disabilities;
9. Mental health proceedings;
10. Termination of parental rights; and
11. Adoption.

Commentary

The child's interests may be served through proceedings not connected with the case in which the child's attorney is participating. In such cases the lawyer may be able to secure assistance for the child by filing or participating in other actions.[26] With an older child or a child with involved parents, the child's attorney may not need court authority to pursue other services. For instance, federal law allows the parent to control special education. A Unified Child and Family Court Model would allow for consistency of representation between related court proceedings, such as mental health or juvenile justice.

D-13. Obligations after Disposition. The child's attorney should seek to ensure continued representation of the child at all further hearings, including at administrative or judicial actions that result in changes to the child's placement or services, so long as the court maintains its jurisdiction.

Commentary

Representing a child should reflect the passage of time and the changing needs of the child. The bulk of the child's attorney's work often comes after the initial hearing, including ongoing permanency planning issues, six-month reviews, case plan reviews, issues of termination, and so forth. The average length of stay in foster care is over five years in some jurisdictions. Often a child's case workers, therapists, other service providers or even placements change while the case is still pending. Different judges may hear various phases of the case. The child's attorney may be the only source of continuity for the child. Such continuity not only provides the child with a stable point of contact, but also may represent the institutional memory of case facts and procedural history for the agency and court. The child's attorney should stay in touch with the child, third party caretakers, caseworkers, and service providers throughout the term of appointment to ensure that the child's needs are met and that the case moves quickly to an appropriate resolution.

Generally, it is preferable for the lawyer to remain involved so long as the case is pending to enable the child's interest to be addressed from the child's perspective at all stages. Like the Juvenile Justice Standards, these Abuse and Neglect Standards require ongoing appointment and active representation as long as the court retains jurisdiction over the child. To the extent that these are separate proceedings in some jurisdictions, the child's attorney should seek reappointment.

Where reappointment is not feasible, the child's attorney should provide records and information about the case and cooperate with the successor to ensure continuity of representation.

E. Post-Hearing

E-1. Review of Court's Order. The child's attorney should review all written orders to ensure that they conform with the court's verbal orders and statutorily required findings and notices.

E-2. Communicate Order to Child. The child's attorney should discuss the order and its consequences with the child.

Commentary
The child is entitled to understand what the court has done and what that means to the child, at least with respect to those portions of the order that directly affect the child. Children may assume that orders are final and not subject to change. Therefore, the lawyer should explain whether the order may be modified at another hearing, or whether the actions of the parties may affect how the order is carried out. For example, an order may permit the agency to return the child to the parent if certain goals are accomplished.

E-3. Implementation. The child's attorney should monitor the implementation of the court's orders and communicate to the responsible agency and, if necessary, the court, any non-compliance.

Commentary
The lawyer should ensure that services are provided and that the court's orders are implemented in a complete and timely fashion. In order to address problems with implementation, the lawyer should stay in touch with the child, caseworker, third party caretakers, and service providers between review hearings. The lawyer should consider filing any necessary motions, including those for civil or criminal contempt, to compel implementation.[27]

F. Appeal

F-1. Decision to Appeal. The child's attorney should consider and discuss with the child, as developmentally appropriate, the possibility of an appeal. If after such consultation, the child wishes to appeal the order, and the appeal has merit, the lawyer should take all steps necessary to perfect the appeal and seek appropriate temporary orders or extraordinary writs necessary to protect the interests of the child during the pendency of the appeal.

Commentary
The lawyer should explain to the child not only the legal possibility of an appeal, but also the ramifications of filing an appeal, including the potential for delaying implementation of services or placement options. The lawyer should also explain whether the trial court's orders will be stayed pending appeal and what the agency and trial court may do pending a final decision.

F-2. Withdrawal. If the child's attorney determines that an appeal would be frivolous or that he or she lacks the necessary experience or expertise to handle the appeal, the lawyer should notify the court and seek to be discharged or replaced.

F-3. Participation in Appeal. The child's attorney should participate in an appeal filed by another party unless discharged.

Commentary
The child's attorney should take a position in any appeal filed by the parent, agency, or other party. In some jurisdictions, the lawyer's appointment does not include representation on appeal. If the child's interests are affected by the issues raised in the appeal, the lawyer should seek an appointment on appeal or seek appointment of appellate counsel to represent the child's position in the appeal.

F-4. Conclusion of Appeal. When the decision is received, the child's attorney should explain the outcome of the case to the child.

Commentary
As with other court decisions, the lawyer should explain in terms the child can understand the nature and consequences of the appellate decision. In addition, the lawyer should explain whether there are further appellate remedies and what more, if anything, will be done in the trial court following the decision.

F-5. Cessation of Representation. The child's attorney should discuss the end of the legal representation and determine what contacts, if any, the child's attorney and the child will continue to have.

Commentary
When the representation ends, the child's lawyer should explain in a developmentally appropriate manner why the representation is ending and how the child can obtain assistance in the future should it become necessary. It is important for there to be closure between the child and the lawyer.

PART II: ENHANCING THE JUDICIAL ROLE IN CHILD REPRESENTATION

Preface

Enhancing the legal representation provided by court-appointed lawyers for children has long been a special concern of the American Bar Association.[28] Yet, no matter how carefully a bar association, legislature, or court defines the duties of lawyers representing children, practice will only improve if judicial administrators and trial judges play a stronger role in the selection, training, oversight, and prompt payment of court-appointed lawyers in child abuse/neglect and child custody/visitation cases.

The importance of the court's role in helping assure competent representation of children is noted in the *Juvenile Justice Standards Relating to Court Organization and Administration* (1980) which state in the Commentary to 3.4D that effective representation of parties is "essential" and that the presiding judge of a court "might need to use his or her position to achieve" it. In its *Resource Guidelines: Improving Court Practice in Child Abuse and Neglect Cases* (1995), the National Council of Juvenile and Family Court Judges stated, "Juvenile and family courts should take active steps to ensure that the parties in child abuse and neglect cases have access to competent representation. . . ." In jurisdictions which engage nonlawyers to represent a child's interests, the court should ensure they have access to legal representation.

These Abuse and Neglect Standards, like the Resource Guidelines, recognize that the courts have a great ability to influence positively the quality of counsel through setting judicial prerequisites for lawyer appointments including requirements for experience and training, imposing sanctions for violation of standards (such as terminating a lawyer's appointment to represent a specific child, denying further appointments, or even fines or referrals to the state bar committee for professional responsibility). The following standards are intended to assist the judiciary in using its authority to accomplish the goal of quality representation for all children before the court in abuse/neglect related proceedings.

G. The Court's Role in Structuring Child Representation

G-1. Assuring Independence of the Child's Attorney. The child's attorney should be independent from the court, court services, the parties, and the state.

Commentary

To help assure that the child's attorney is not compromised in his or her independent action, these standards propose that the child's lawyer be independent from other participants in the litigation. "Independence" does not mean that a lawyer may not receive payment from a court, a government entity (e.g., program funding from social services or justice agencies), or even from a parent, relative, or other adult so long as the lawyer retains the full authority for independent action. For ethical conflict reasons, however, lawyers should never accept compensation as retained counsel for the child from a parent accused of abusing or neglecting the child. The child's attorney should not prejudge the case. The concept of independence includes being free from prejudice and other limitations to uncompromised representation.

Juvenile Justice Standard 2.1(d) states that plans for providing counsel for children "must be designed to guarantee the professional independence of counsel and the integrity of the lawyer-client relationship." The Commentary strongly asserts there is "no justification for . . . judicial preference" to compromise a lawyer's relationship with the child client and notes the "willingness of some judges to direct lawyers' performance and thereby compromise their independence."

G-2. Establishing Uniform Representation Rules. The administrative office for the state trial, family, or juvenile court system should cause to be published and disseminated to all relevant courts a set of uniform, written rules and procedures for court-appointed lawyers for minor children.

Commentary

Although uniform rules of court to govern the processing of various types of child-related judicial proceedings have become common, it is still rare for those rules to address comprehensively the manner and scope of representation for children. Many lawyers representing children are unclear as to the court's expectations. Courts in different communities, or even judges within the same court, may have differing views regarding the manner of child representation. These standards promote statewide uniformity by calling for written publication and distribution of state rules and procedures for the child's attorney.

G-3. Enhancing Lawyer Relationships with Other Court Connected Personnel. Courts that operate or utilize Court Appointed Special Advocate (CASA) and other nonlawyer guardians ad litem, and courts that administer nonjudicial foster care review bodies, should assure that these programs and the individuals performing those roles are trained to understand the role of the child's attorney. There needs to be effective coordination of their efforts with the activities of the child's attorney, and they need to involve the child's attorney in their work. The court should require that reports from agencies be prepared and presented to the parties in a timely fashion.

Commentary
Many courts now regularly involve nonlawyer advocates for children in various capacities. Some courts also operate programs that, outside of the courtroom, review the status of children in foster care or other out-of-home placements. It is critical that these activities are appropriately linked to the work of the child's attorney, and that the court through training, policies, and protocols helps assure that those performing the nonlegal tasks (1) understand the importance and elements of the role of the child's attorney, and (2) work cooperatively with such lawyers. The court should keep abreast of all the different representatives involved with the child, the attorney, social worker for government or private agency, CASA volunteer, guardian ad litem, school mediator, counselors, etc.

H. The Court's Role in Appointing the Child's Attorney

H-1. Timing of Appointments. The child's attorney should be appointed immediately after the earliest of:

1. The involuntary removal of the child for placement due to allegations of neglect, abuse or abandonment;
2. The filing of a petition alleging child abuse and neglect, for review of foster care placement, or for termination of parental rights; or
3. Allegations of child maltreatment, based upon sufficient cause, are made by a party in the context of proceedings that were not originally initiated by a petition alleging child maltreatment.

Commentary
These Abuse and Neglect Standards take the position that courts must assure the appointment of a lawyer for a child as soon as practical (ideally, on the day the court first has jurisdiction over the case, and hopefully, no later than the next business day). The three situations are described separately because:

1. A court may authorize, or otherwise learn of, a child's removal from home prior to the time a formal petition is instituted.

Lawyer representation of (and, ideally, contact with) the child prior to the initial court hearing following removal (which in some cases may be several days) is important to protect the child's interests;

2. Once a petition has been filed by a government agency (or, where authorized, by a hospital or other agency with child protection responsibilities), for any reason related to a child's need for protection, the child should have prompt access to a lawyer; and

3. There are cases (such as custody, visitation, and guardianship disputes and family-related abductions of children) where allegations, with sufficient cause, of serious physical abuse, sexual molestation, or severe neglect of a child are presented to the court not by a government agency (i.e., child protective services) but by a parent, guardian, or other relative. The need of a child for competent, independent representation by a lawyer is just as great in situation (3) as with cases in areas (1) and (2).

H-2. Entry of Compensation Orders. At the time the court appoints a child's attorney, it should enter a written order addressing compensation and expense costs for that lawyer, unless these are otherwise formally provided for by agreement or contract with the court, or through another government agency.

Commentary
Compensation and expense reimbursement of individual lawyers should be addressed in a specific written court order and is based on a need for all lawyers representing maltreated children to have a uniform understanding of how they will be paid. Commentary to Section 2.1(b) of the Juvenile Justice Standards observes that it is common for court-appointed lawyers to be confused about the availability of reimbursement of expenses for case-related work.

H-3. Immediate Provision of Access. Unless otherwise provided for, the court should upon appointment of a child's attorney, enter an order authorizing that lawyer access between the child and the lawyer and to all privileged information regarding the child, without the necessity of a further release. The authorization should include, but not be limited to: social services, psychiatric, psychological treatment, drug and alcohol treatment, medical, evaluation, law enforcement, and school records.

Commentary
Because many service providers do not understand or recognize the nature of the role of the lawyer for the child or that person's importance in the court proceeding, these standards call for the routine use of a written court order that clarifies the lawyer's right to contact with their child client and perusal of child-related records. Parents, other caretakers, or government social service agencies should not unreasonably interfere with a lawyer's ability to have face-to-face contact with the child client nor to obtain relevant information about the child's social services, education, mental health, etc. Such interference disrupts the lawyer's ability to control the representation and undermines his or her independence as the child's legal representative.

H-4. Lawyer Eligibility for and Method of Appointment. Where the court makes individual appointment of counsel, unless impractical, before making the appointment, the court should determine that the lawyer has been trained in representation of children and skilled in litigation (or is working under the supervision of a lawyer who is skilled in litigation). Whenever possible, the trial judge should ensure that the child's attorney has had sufficient training in child advocacy and is familiar with these standards. The trial judge should also ensure that (unless there is specific reason to appoint a specific lawyer because of their special qualifications related to the case, or where a lawyer's current caseload would prevent them from adequately handling the case) individual lawyers are appointed from the ranks of eligible members of the bar under a fair, systematic, and sequential appointment plan.

Commentary
Juvenile Justice Standard 2.2(c) provides that where counsel is assigned by the court, this lawyer should be drawn from "an adequate pool of competent attorneys." In general, such competency can only be gained through relevant continuing legal education and practice-related experience. Those standards also promote the use of a rational court appointment process drawing from the ranks of qualified lawyers. The Abuse and Neglect Standards reject the concept of ad hoc appointments of counsel that are made without regard to prior training or practice.

H-5. Permitting Child to Retain a Lawyer. The court should permit the child to be represented by a retained private lawyer if it determines that this lawyer is the child's independent choice, and such counsel should be substituted for the appointed lawyer. A person with a legitimate interest in the child's welfare may retain private counsel for the child and/or pay for such representation, and that person should be permitted to serve as the child's attorney, subject to approval of the court. Such approval should not be given if the child opposes the lawyer's representation or if the court determines that there will be a conflict of interest. The court should make it clear that the person paying for the retained lawyer does not have the right to direct the representation of the child or to receive privileged information about the case from the lawyer.

Commentary
Although such representation is rare, there are situations where a child, or someone acting on a child's behalf, seeks out legal representation and wishes that this lawyer, rather than one appointed by the court under the normal appointment process, be recognized as the sole legal representative of the child. Sometimes, judges have refused to accept the formal appearances filed by such retained lawyers. These standards propose to permit, under carefully scrutinized conditions, the substitution of a court-appointed lawyer with the retained counsel for a child.

I. The Court's Role in Lawyer Training

I-1. Judicial Involvement in Lawyer Training. Trial judges who are regularly involved in child-related matters should participate in training for the child's attorney conducted by the courts, the bar, or any other group.

Commentary
Juvenile Justice Standard 2.1 indicates that it is the responsibility of the courts (among others) to ensure that competent counsel are available to represent children before the courts. That Standard further suggests that lawyers should "be encouraged" to qualify themselves for participation in child-related cases "through formal training." The Abuse and Neglect Standards go further by suggesting that judges should personally take part in educational programs, whether or not the court conducts them. The National Council of Juvenile and Family Court Judges has suggested that courts can play in important role in training lawyers in child abuse and neglect cases, and that judges and judicial officers can volunteer to provide training and publications for continuing legal education seminars.[29]

I-2. Content of Lawyer Training. The appropriate state administrative office of the trial, family, or juvenile courts should provide educational programs, live or on tape, on the role of a child's attorney. At a minimum, the requisite training should include:

1. Information about relevant federal and state laws and agency regulations;
2. Information about relevant court decisions and court rules;
3. Overview of the court process and key personnel in child-related litigation;
4. Description of applicable guidelines and standards for representation;
5. Focus on child development, needs, and abilities;
6. Information on the multidisciplinary input required in child-related cases, including information on local experts who can provide consultation and testimony on the reasonableness and appropriateness of efforts made to safely maintain the child in his or her home;
7. Information concerning family dynamics and dysfunction including substance abuse, and the use of kinship care;
8. Information on accessible child welfare, family preservation, medical, educational, and mental health resources for child clients and their families, including placement, evaluation/diagnostic, and treatment services; the structure of agencies providing such services as well as provisions and constraints related to agency payment for services; and
9. Provision of written material (e.g., representation manuals, checklists, sample forms), including listings of useful material available from other sources.

Commentary

The Abuse and Neglect Standards take the position that it is not enough that judges mandate the training of lawyers, or that judges participate in such training. Rather, they call upon the courts to play a key role in training by actually sponsoring (e.g., funding) training opportunities. The pivotal nature of the judiciary's role in educating lawyers means that courts may, on appropriate occasions, stop the hearing of cases on days when training is held so that both lawyers and judges may freely attend without docket conflicts. The required elements of training are based on a review of well-regarded lawyer training offered throughout the country, Resource Guidelines, and many existing manuals that help guide lawyers in representing children.

I-3. Continuing Training for Lawyers. The court system should also assure that there are periodic opportunities for lawyers who have taken the "basic" training to receive continuing and "new developments" training.

Commentary
Many courts and judicial organizations recognize that rapid changes occur because of new federal and state legislation, appellate court decisions, systemic reforms, and responses to professional literature. Continuing education opportunities are critical to maintain a high level of performance. These standards call for courts to afford these "advanced" or "periodic" training to lawyers who represent children in abuse and neglect related cases.

I-4. Provision of Mentorship Opportunities. Courts should provide individual court-appointed lawyers who are new to child representation the opportunity to practice under the guidance of a senior lawyer mentor.

Commentary
In addition to training, particularly for lawyers who work as sole practitioners or in firms that do not specialize in child representation, courts can provide a useful mechanism to help educate new lawyers for children by pairing them with more experienced advocates. One specific thing courts can do is to provide lawyers new to representing children with the opportunity to be assisted by more experienced lawyers in their jurisdiction. Some courts actually require lawyers to "second chair" cases before taking an appointment to a child abuse or neglect case.[30]

J. The Court's Role in Lawyer Compensation

J-1. Assuring Adequate Compensation. A child's attorney should receive adequate and timely compensation throughout the term of appointment that reflects the complexity of the case and includes both in court and out-of-court preparation, participation in case reviews and post-dispositional hearings, and involvement in appeals. To the extent that the court arranges for child representation through contract or agreement with a program in which lawyers represent children, the court should assure that the rate of payment for these legal services is commensurate with the fees paid to equivalently experienced individual court-appointed lawyers who have similar qualifications and responsibilities.

Commentary
Juvenile Justice Standards 2.1(b) recognize that lawyers for children should be entitled to reasonable compensation for both time and services performed "according to prevailing professional standards," which takes into account the "skill required to perform . . . properly," and which considers the need for the lawyer to perform both counseling and resource identification/evaluation activities. The Resource Guidelines, at 22, state that it is "necessary to provide reasonable compensation" for improved lawyer representation of children and that where necessary judges should "urge state legislatures and local governing bodies to provide sufficient funding" for quality legal representation.

Because some courts currently compensate lawyers only for time spent in court at the adjudicative or initial disposition stage of cases, these standards clarify that compensation is to be provided for out-of-court preparation time, as well as for the lawyer's involvement in case reviews and appeals. "Out-of-court preparation" may include, for example, a lawyer's participation in social services or school case conferences relating to the client.

These standards also call for the level of compensation where lawyers are working under contract with the court to provide child representation to be comparable with what experienced individual counsel would receive from the court. Although courts may, and are encouraged to, seek high quality child representation through enlistment of special children's law offices, law firms, and other programs, the motive should not be a significantly different (i.e., lower) level of financial compensation for the lawyers who provide the representation.

J-2. Supporting Associated Costs. The child's attorney should have access to (or be provided with reimbursement for) experts, investigative services, paralegals, research costs, and other services, such as copying medical records, long distance phone calls, service of process, and transcripts of hearings as requested.

Commentary
The *Abuse and Neglect Standards* expand upon *Juvenile Justice Standards* 2.1(c), which recognizes that a child's attorney should have access to "investigatory, expert and other nonlegal services" as a fundamental part of providing competent representation.

J-3. Reviewing Payment Requests. The trial judge should review requests for compensation for reasonableness based upon the complexity of the case and the hours expended.

Commentary
These standards implicitly reject the practice of judges arbitrarily "cutting down" the size of lawyer requests for compensation and would limit a judge's ability to reduce the amount of a per/case payment request from a child's attorney unless the request is deemed unreasonable based upon two factors: case complexity and time spent.

J-4. Keeping Compensation Levels Uniform. Each state should set a uniform level of compensation for lawyers appointed by the courts to represent children. Any per/hour level of compensation should be the same for all representation of children in all types of child abuse and neglect-related proceedings.

Commentary
These standards implicitly reject the concept (and practice) of different courts within a state paying different levels of compensation for lawyers representing children. They call for a uniform approach, established on a statewide basis, towards the setting of payment guidelines.

K. The Court's Role in Record Access by Lawyers

K-1. Authorizing Lawyer Access. The court should enter an order in child abuse and neglect cases authorizing the child's attorney access to all privileged information regarding the child, without the necessity for a further release.

Commentary
This Standard requires uniform judicial assistance to remove a common barrier to effective representation, i.e., administrative denial of access to significant records concerning the child. The language supports the universal issuance of broadly-worded court orders that grant a child's attorney full access to information (from individuals) or records (from agencies) concerning the child.

K-2. Providing Broad Scope Orders. The authorization order granting the child's attorney access to records should include social services, psychiatric, psychological treatment, drug and alcohol treatment, medical, evaluation, law enforcement, school, and other records relevant to the case.

Commentary
This Standard further elaborates upon the universal application that the court's access order should be given, by listing examples of the most common agency records that should be covered by the court order.

L. The Court's Role in Assuring Reasonable Lawyer Caseloads

L-1. Controlling Lawyer Caseloads. Trial court judges should control the size of court-appointed caseloads of individual lawyers representing children, the caseloads of government agency-funded lawyers for children, or court contracts/agreements with lawyers for such representation. Courts should take steps to assure that lawyers appointed to represent children, or lawyers otherwise providing such representation, do not have such a large open number of cases that they are unable to abide by Part I of these standards.

Commentary
The Abuse and Neglect Standards go further than Juvenile Justice Standards 2.2(b) which recognize the "responsibility of every defender office to ensure that its personnel can offer prompt, full, and effective counseling and representation to each (child) client" and that it "should not accept more assignments than its staff can adequately discharge" by specifically calling upon the courts to help keep lawyer caseloads from getting out of control. The Commentary to 2.2(b) indicates that: Caseloads must not be exceeded where to do so would "compel lawyers to forego the extensive fact investigation required in both contested and uncontested cases, or to be less than scrupulously careful in preparation for trial, or to forego legal research necessary to develop a theory of representation." We would add: ". . . or to monitor the implementation of court orders and agency case plans in order to help assure permanency for the child."

L-2. Taking Supportive Caseload Actions. If judges or court administrators become aware that individual lawyers are close to, or exceeding, the levels suggested in these standards, they should take one or more of the following steps:

1. Expand, with the aid of the bar and children's advocacy groups, the size of the list from which appointments are made;
2. Alert relevant government or private agency administrators that their lawyers have an excessive caseload problem;
3. Recruit law firms or special child advocacy law programs to engage in child representation;
4. Review any court contracts/agreements for child representation and amend them accordingly, so that additional lawyers can be compensated for case representation time; and

5. Alert state judicial, executive, and legislative branch leaders that excessive caseloads jeopardize the ability of lawyers to competently represent children pursuant to state-approved guidelines, and seek funds for increasing the number of lawyers available to represent children.

Commentary
This Standard provides courts with a range of possible actions when individual lawyer caseloads appear to be inappropriately high.

ACKNOWLEDGMENTS

These standards were drafted by Howard Davidson, Director, ABA Center on Children and the Law, with the assistance of the ABA Family Law Section. They were approved by the ABA House of Delegates in 1996.

APPENDIX

Previous American Bar Association Policies Related to Legal Representation of Abused and Neglected Children

GUARDIANS AD LITEM
FEBRUARY 1992

BE IT RESOLVED, that the American Bar Association urges:

1. Every state and territory to meet the full intent of the Federal Child Abuse Prevention and Treatment Act, whereby every child in the United States who is the subject of a civil child protection related judicial proceedings will be represented at all stages of these proceedings by a fully-trained, monitored, and evaluated guardian ad litem in addition to appointed legal counsel.
2. That state, territory and local bar associations and law schools become involved in setting standards of practice for such guardians ad litem, clarify the ethical responsibilities of these individuals and establish minimum ethical performance requirements for their work, and provide comprehensive multidisciplinary training for all who serve as such guardians ad litem.

3. That in every state and territory, where judges are given discretion to appoint a guardian ad litem in private child custody and visitation related proceedings, the bench and bar jointly develop guidelines to aid judges in determining when such an appointment is necessary to protect the best interests of the child.

COURT-APPOINTED SPECIAL ADVOCATES
AUGUST 1989

BE IT RESOLVED, that the American Bar Association endorses the concept of utilizing carefully selected, well trained lay volunteers, Court Appointed Special Advocates, in addition to providing attorney representation, in dependency proceedings to assist the court in determining what is in the best interests of abused and neglected children.

BE IT FURTHER RESOLVED, that the American Bar Association encourages its members to support the development of CASA programs in their communities.

COUNSEL FOR CHILDREN ENHANCEMENT
FEBRUARY 1987

BE IT RESOLVED, that the American Bar Association requests State and local bar associations to determine the extent to which statutory law and court rules in their States guarantee the right to counsel for children in juvenile court proceedings; and

BE IT FURTHER RESOLVED, that State and local bar associations are urged to actively participate and support amendments to the statutory law and court rules in their State to bring them in to compliance with the Institute of Judicial Administration/American Bar Association Standards Relating to Counsel for Private Parties; and

BE IT FURTHER RESOLVED, that State and local bar associations are requested to ascertain the extent to which, irrespective of the language in their State statutory laws and court rules, counsel is in fact provided for children in juvenile court proceedings and the extent to which the quality of representation is consistent with the standards and policies of the American Bar Association; and

BE IT FURTHER RESOLVED, that State and local bar associations are urged to actively support programs of training and education to ensure that lawyers practicing in juvenile court are aware of the American Bar Association's standards relating to representation of children and provide advocacy which meets those standards.

BAR ASSOCIATION AND ATTORNEY ACTION
FEBRUARY 1984

BE IT RESOLVED, that the American Bar Association urges the members of the legal profession, as well as state and local bar associations, to respond to the needs of children by directing attention to issues affecting children including, but not limited to: . . . (7) establishment of guardian ad litem programs.

BAR AND ATTORNEY INVOLVEMENT IN CHILD
PROTECTION CASES
AUGUST 1981

BE IT RESOLVED, that the American Bar Association encourages individual attorneys and state and local bar organizations to work more actively to improve the handling of cases involving abused and neglected children as well as children in foster care. Specifically, attorneys should form appropriate committees and groups within the bar to . . . work to assure quality legal representation for children. . . .

JUVENILE JUSTICE STANDARDS
FEBRUARY 1979

BE IT RESOLVED, that the American Bar Association adopt (the volume of the) Standards for Juvenile Justice (entitled) Counsel for Private Parties. . .

NOTES

1. *See* Binder, David A. & Susan C. Price. *Legal Interviewing and Counseling: A Client-Centered Approach*, 1977.
2. *See* Graffam Walker, Anne. *Handbook on Questioning Children: A Linguistic Perspective.* Washington, DC: ABA Center on Children and the Law, 1994.
3. *See* National Council of Juvenile and Family Court Judges. *Resource Guidelines: Improving Court Practice in Child Abuse & Neglect Cases*, 1995, 23.

4. *Compare* Alaska Bar Assoc. Ethics Op. #854 (1985) (lawyer-client privilege does not apply when the lawyer is appointed to be child's guardian ad litem) with *Bentley v. Bentley*, 448 N.Y.S.2d 559 (App. Div. 1982) (communication between minor children and guardian ad litem in divorce custody case is entitled to lawyer-client privilege).

5. *See* Arizona State Bar Committee on Rules of Professional Conduct, Opinion No. 86-13 (1986).

6. *See, e.g.*, Buchanan, Allen E. & Dan W. Brock. *Deciding for Others: The Ethics of Surrogate Decision Making*, 1989, 217.

7. *See* ER 1.2(d), Model Rules of Professional Conduct, DR 7-102(A)(7), Model Code of Professional Responsibility.

8. *See* ER 1.6(b), Model Rules of Professional Conduct.

9. *See* ER 1.6(c), Model Rules of Professional Conduct, DR 4-101(C)(3), Model Code of Professional Responsibility.

10. *See* DR-7-101(A)(1), Model Code of Professional Responsibility.

11. *See generally* Garbarino, James & Frances M. Stott. *What Children Can Tell Us: Eliciting, Interpreting, and Evaluating Critical Information from Children*, 1992.

12. *Id.*

13. *See Resource Guidelines*, 1995, 23.

14. *Id.*

15. *Id.*

16. *Id.*

17. *See generally* Jacobs, Thomas A. *Children and the Law: Rights and Obligations*, 1995; *Legal Rights of Children*, 2d ed. Edited by Donald T. Kramer, 1994.

18. *See* Haralambie, Ann M. *The Child's Attorney: A Guide to Representing Children in Custody, Adoption, and Protection Cases*, 1994, ch. 4.

19. *See* Myers, John E.B. *Evidence in Child Abuse and Neglect Cases*, 2, ch. 8, 1992.

20. *See generally* Saywitz, Karen. "Children in Court: Principles of Child Development for Judicial Application." In *A Judicial Primer on Child Sexual Abuse*, edited by Josephine Bulkley & Claire Sandt, 1994, 15.

21. *See generally* Saywitz, id.; *Child Victims, Child Witnesses: Understanding and Improving Testimony*. Edited by Gail S. Goodman & Bette L. Bottoms, 1993; Haralambie, Ann. *Handling Child Custody, Abuse, And Adoption Cases*, 2d ed.. 1993, 24.09, 24.22; Myers, 1992, Vol. 1, ch 2; Matthews, Ellen & Karen Saywitz, *Child Victim Witness Manual*, 12/1 C.J.E.R.J. 40, 1992.

22. *See* Walker, 1994; *see also supra* A-3 Commentary.

23. *See* Haralambie, 1993, 24.17.

24. *See* Parley, Louis I. "Representing Children in Custody Litigation." *Journal of the Academy of Matrimonial Law* 11, 45, 48, Winter 1993.

25. *See generally* Saywitz, 1994, 15; *Child Victims*, 1993; Haralambie, 1993; Myers, 1992; Matthews & Saywitz, 1992.

26. *See, e.g.*, In re Appeal in Pima County Juvenile Action No. S-113432, 872 P.2d 1240 (Ariz. Ct. App. 1994).

27. *See Resource Guidelines*, 1995, 23.

28. *See, e.g.*, *Juvenile Justice Standards Relating to Counsel for Private Parties*, 1979; ABA Policy Resolutions on Representation of Children, *see* Appendix.

29. *See Resource Guidelines*, 1995, 22.

30. *Id.*

Standards of Practice for Lawyers Representing Child Welfare Agencies

AUGUST 2004

INTRODUCTION

The purpose of these standards is to improve the quality of child welfare agency representation and uniformity of practice throughout the country. Many agency attorneys who read these standards may recognize their practice in this document. The standards are meant to improve practice, but also to be realistically attainable by individual jurisdictions. The standards were written with the help of a committee of practicing agency attorneys and child welfare professionals from different jurisdictions in the country. With their help, the standards were written with the difficulties of day-to-day practice in mind, but also with the goal of raising the quality of representation as much as possible. While local adjustments may be necessary to incorporate these standards into practice, jurisdictions should strive to meet the fundamental principles and spirit of the standards.

The standards are divided into the following five categories:

(a) Definitions
(b) Role of the Agency Attorney, including a list of the Basic
    Obligations
(c) Fulfilling the Obligations
(d) Ethical and Practice Considerations

(e) Administrative Responsibilities, including a list of the Basic Obligations of an Agency Attorney Manager

Section B and E-1 contain lists of the standards for agency attorneys and agency attorney managers for quick reference. These standards are explained in more detail in the rest of the document. Within sections C, D, and E there are "black letter" standards, or requirements written in bold. Following the black letter are "actions." These actions provide additional discussion on how to fulfill the standard; implementing each standard requires the accompanying action. After the action is "commentary" or a discussion of why the standard is necessary and how it should be applied. In some instances, a standard did not need further explanation, so there is no action or commentary attached. A number of the standards relate to specific sections of the Model Rules of Professional Conduct, and the Model Rules are referenced in these standards.

Representing a child welfare agency is a difficult yet important job. There are many, sometimes conflicting, responsibilities. These standards are intended to help the agency attorney prioritize his or her duties and manage the practice in a way that will benefit the agency and ultimately the children and families for whom the agency provides services.

A. Definitions

A-1. Agency. The state or county child welfare agency that is charged with protecting and caring for children suspected or found to be abused or neglected and providing services to the child's family. The agency investigates reports of child abuse and neglect, provides preventative services to families and takes custody of children and oversees their placement in foster care. If a child is placed in foster care, the agency works with the family to reunite the child or achieve another permanency outcome for the child. The agency may also work with unruly children, status offenders, or delinquent children.

Commentary
When applying or adapting these standards locally, it is important to define this term in a jurisdiction-specific manner. There are a wide range of names for child welfare agencies such as the Department of Human Services (DHS), the Department of Social Services (DSS), Children Youth and Families.

A-2. Agency Attorney. An attorney who is an employee or contractor with the government who is charged with the responsibility of initiating proceedings on behalf of the government or the people to protect abused and neglected children.

Commentary
Defining this term in a jurisdiction-specific manner is critical. Everyone should be clear on which attorneys are covered by the practice standards and who the client is.

A-3. Client. A person or entity who employs an attorney or counselor to appear in court, advise, assist and defend in legal proceedings. The client is the entity to which the agency attorney is responsible.[1]

Commentary
State law varies concerning the agency attorney's client. Generally, it is either the child welfare agency itself, or "the people" in a prosecutorial model of representation. *See* section B-1 for further discussion. The attorney must understand who the client is and the parameters of the representation.

A-4. Abuse and Neglect Proceedings. A category of legal proceedings designed to protect maltreated or endangered children that is generally initiated by the government. This group of cases may involve such proceedings as abuse, neglect, dependency, or abandonment cases. It typically involves, among other things, adjudications, case reviews, permanency hearings, termination of parental rights, adoption, and, in some states, guardianship and custody. "Family Drug Courts" and other specialty dockets, if they handle dependency cases, should be included in this category.

Commentary
State law and procedure will dictate the names and types of cases that fall in this category. Many states use different terminology to describe these cases such as "child in need of assistance," "dependency," "abuse and neglect."

B. Role

B-1. Models of Agency Attorney Representation. There are two basic models of agency representation:
  Agency Representation Model: Under this model, the agency attorney represents the agency as a legal entity, much the same as in-house

counsel's role in representing a corporation.[2] The attorney could be an employee of the agency or of another governmental body, but the agency is clearly the defined client. Some of the benefits of this model include:

- reliance on agency's familiarity with a child and family in decision making;
- value placed on the agency's expertise in making decisions regarding the safety, permanency and well-being of children and on the lawyer's legal expertise on legal matters;
- consistent decision making and interpretation of laws;
- legal action supported by caseworker opinion, thus boosting caseworker credibility in court, for example, in deciding when to file an initial petition; and,
- the attorney is very familiar with the agency and its practices and policies.

One drawback to this model is that caseworkers may believe the attorney represents them personally rather than the agency as a whole. While in practice this may generally be true because the caseworker is the voice for the agency in court, the agency attorney must clearly communicate that he or she represents the agency as an entity and should use the conflict resolution system (refer to D-1 below) when the caseworker's opinion varies from agency policy or the attorney has reason to question the caseworker's decision.[3]

Prosecutorial Model: Under this model, an elected or appointed attorney (or the attorneys working for this individual), often a district attorney or county attorney, files petitions and appears in court on behalf of the agency, and represents the state or "the people" of the jurisdiction. This may mean the elected attorney may override the views of the agency in court. One positive aspect of this model is that the attorney may be more in tune with the wishes and beliefs of the community and how the community feels about handling child welfare cases. Concerns with this model include:

- the caseworker is often the only party in court without an attorney speaking for him or her;
- the caseworker's expertise may be ignored, as the attorney has the ultimate say;
- the attorney may be handling all the business for the community and therefore not be able to specialize in child welfare law;
- political agendas may play a large role in decision-making;

- the agency as a whole may not be getting legal advice on policy issues;
- the attorney's personal beliefs about issues such as permanency rather than caseworker expertise dictate what will happen for a child; and,
- potential conflicts of interest may arise, such as when the prosecutor is pursuing a delinquency petition against a child who is in the agency's custody.[4]

Commentary

No matter what the model of representation, it is essential that the agency attorney and agency communicate clearly about which model applies. Each should understand who makes the ultimate decisions in different circumstances and there should be a method for resolving a decision-making conflict, should it arise. In each model, there will be times when decision-making roles are unclear and open communication is essential. The agency attorney and agency should understand the attorney's role and responsibilities concerning advising and protecting the agency on liability issues. Additionally, no matter which representation model is used, the agency attorney must understand his or her role with respect to private agencies with whom the agency contracts. The most important issues are that children are safe, their needs are met, and their families are treated fairly.

The drafting committee of these standards recommends the agency representation model. However, state legislation may dictate what model each attorney must follow. States are cautioned against developing hybrid models which incorporate elements of both the agency model and the prosecution model of representation because of the inherent risks of conflict such hybrid models could create for attorneys. These standards apply to all agency attorneys, no matter what model they use for representation.

B-2. Basic Obligations. The agency attorney shall:

General[5]

1. Fully understand and comply with all relevant federal and state laws, regulations, policies, and rules;
2. Promote timely hearings and reduce case continuances;
3. Protect and promote the agency's credibility;
4. Cooperate and communicate on a regular basis with other professionals and parties in a case, including the client/agency;[6]

Advise and Counsel[7]

    5. Counsel the client/agency about all legal matters related to individual cases as well as policy issues and periodically monitor cases;

Court Preparation[8]

    6. Develop a case theory and strategy to follow at hearings and negotiations;

    7. Prepare or help prepare the initial petition and all subsequent pleadings;

    8. Timely file all pleadings, motions, and briefs;

    9. Obtain all documents and information needed, including copies of all pleadings and relevant notices filed by other parties;

  10. Participate in all depositions, negotiations, discovery, pretrial conferences, mediation sessions (when appropriate), and hearings;

  11. Participate in settlement negotiations and attempt speedy resolution of the case, when appropriate;

  12. Develop a case timeline and tickler system;

  13. Subpoena and prepare all witnesses, including the client;

  14. Ensure proper notice is provided to all parties and necessary caretakers;

Hearings

  15. Attend and prepare for all hearings;

  16. Prepare and make all appropriate motions and evidentiary objections;

  17. Present case in chief, present and cross-examine witnesses, prepare and present exhibits;

  18. In jurisdictions in which a jury trial is possible, participate in jury selection and drafting jury instructions;

  19. Request the opportunity to make brief opening and closing arguments when appropriate;

  20. Prepare or help prepare proposed findings of fact, conclusions of law and orders when they will be used in the court's decision;

Post Hearings/Appeals

  21. Follow all court orders pertaining to the attorney for the client/agency;

  22. Review court orders to ensure accuracy and clarity and review with agency when necessary;

23. Take reasonable steps to ensure the agency complies with court orders;
24. Consider and discuss with the agency the possibility of appeal;
25. If a decision is made to appeal, timely file the necessary post-hearing motions and the notice to appeal paperwork;
26. Request an expedited appeal, when feasible, and file all necessary paperwork while the appeal is pending;
27. Communicate the results of the appeal and its implications to the agency/client.

Commentary
This list is not comprehensive but includes key aspects of the agency attorney's role. The agency attorney has many tasks to perform. An initial section of any standards should define these responsibilities.

C. Fulfillment of Obligations

C-1. General:

1. **Fully understand and comply with all relevant federal and state laws, regulations, policies and rules.**

Action
The following laws, at a minimum, are essential for the agency attorney to understand:

- Titles IV-B and IV-E of the Social Security Act, including the Adoption and Safe Families Act (ASFA), 42 U.S.C. §§ 620-679 and the ASFA Regulations, 45 C.F.R. Parts 1355, 1356, 1357
- Child Abuse Prevention Treatment Act (CAPTA), 42 U.S.C. §5101
- Indian Child Welfare Act (ICWA) 25 U.S.C. §§1901-1963, and the ICWA Regulations, 25 C.F.R. Part 23
- Multi-Ethnic Placement Act (MEPA), as amended by the Inter-Ethnic Adoption Provisions of 1996 (MEPA-IEP) 42 U.S.C. § 622 (b)(9) (1998), 42 U.S.C. § 671(a)(18) (1998), 42 U.S.C. §1996b (1998).
- Interstate Compact on Placement of Children (ICPC)
- Foster Care Independence Act of 1999, P.L. 106-169
- Individuals with Disabilities Education Act (IDEA), P.L. 91-230
- Family Education Rights Privacy Act (FERPA), 20 U.S.C. §1232g
- Health Insurance Portability and Accountability Act of 1996 (HIPPA), P. L., 104-192 §264, 42 U.S.C. §1320d-2 (in relevant part)

- All state laws, policies and procedures regarding child abuse and neglect
- State laws concerning privilege and confidentiality, public benefits, education, and disabilities
- State's Rules of Professional Responsibility or other relevant ethics standards

Commentary

The agency attorney, in most instances, files the initial petition with the court and has the burden of proof during court proceedings. Additionally, the agency attorney must advise caseworkers and agency administrators concerning the legality of actions and policies. To best perform these functions, the agency attorney should be an expert in all relevant laws.

2. Promote timely hearings and reduce case continuances.

Action

The agency attorney must be prepared to move cases forward in a timely manner. The agency attorney should only request case continuances in extenuating circumstances. The agency attorney should oppose other parties' requests for continuances absent extenuating circumstances. The agency attorney must be thoroughly prepared for all hearings.

Commentary

Delay in cases slows permanency for children. The agency has a duty to ensure that children do not linger in foster care, and the agency attorney must assist the agency meet this duty. Requesting or agreeing to case continuances should be unusual rather than routine practice.

3. Protect and promote the agency's credibility.

Action

The agency attorney should work with the agency to bring only appropriate cases to the court. The agency attorney should not file frivolous motions or appeals and should counsel caseworkers concerning the legitimacy of positions. The agency attorney should present cases to the court in a professional, knowledgeable manner. The agency attorney should ensure accurate testimony and correct any misstatements in the courtroom. The agency attorney should present a positive image of the agency at community functions and meetings. The agency attorney should be respectful of caseworkers in the courtroom and in the presence of other professionals and parties in a case.

Commentary
The agency must abide by confidentiality laws, and therefore must keep some information private. Without that information, the public may blame the agency on issues concerning controversial cases. Similarly, the agency may make unpopular decisions that it views are in the best interest of the children in the community. The agency attorney should do everything in his or her power to demonstrate the positive aspects of the agency. The agency attorney must thoroughly understand the attorney client confidentiality issue and work diligently to avoid divulging confidential information. The agency attorney should guide the agency to avoid steps that will make it look bad in court and the attorney should protect the caseworkers from humiliation by the judge or other attorneys.

4. Cooperate and communicate on a regular basis with other professionals and parties in a case, including the client/agency.

Action
The agency attorney should have regularly scheduled opportunities to meet with caseworkers and other agency staff. Agency attorneys should treat everyone involved in a case with professional courtesy and should work with everyone to resolve conflict. The agency attorney should have open lines of communication with the prosecutor of related criminal matters. This can be important, for example, in ensuring that probation orders and disposition orders do not conflict, and, where appropriate, are mutually reinforcing (e.g., a visitation order in an abuse and neglect case should not contradict a stay away order from a criminal court).

Commentary
The agency attorney must have all relevant information to effectively try a case. This requires open and ongoing communication with caseworkers and other witnesses. The agency attorney is often the actual or perceived representative of the agency and should present him or herself in a professional manner when before the judge or meeting with other individuals involved in a case. The agency attorney should share relevant information from the case file with other parties in the case, when appropriate.

C-2. Advise and Counsel.

    5. Counsel the client/agency about all legal matters related to individual cases as well as policy issues and periodically monitor cases.

Action

The agency attorney must spend time with caseworkers to prepare individual cases and answer questions. The attorney should explain to the caseworker, in clear language, what is expected to happen before, during and after each hearing. The agency attorney should be available for in-person meetings, telephone calls, and when appropriate, to periodically monitor cases. The agency attorney is not the caseworker supervisor, but rather should monitor to ensure that legal barriers, such as notice and unresolved paternity, are removed. The agency attorney should attend major case staffings when appropriate. The attorney should be aware of any barriers the parents may have to participating in the proposed case plan, such as an inability to read or language barriers, and counsel the agency accordingly. The attorney should be available to agency administrative staff to advise on policy concerns or general issues facing the agency from the court or community.

Commentary

The agency attorney's job extends beyond the courtroom. The attorney should be a counselor as well as litigator. The agency attorney should be available to talk with caseworkers to prepare cases, to provide advice about ongoing concerns, and provide information about policy issues. Open lines of communication between attorneys and caseworkers help ensure caseworkers get answers to questions and attorneys get the information and documents they need. A major case staffing is one in which the attorney or caseworker believes the attorney will be needed to provide advice or one in which a major decision on legal steps or strategies will be decided. The attorney and agency may want to create a policy in advance concerning whether the agency attorney should routinely attend certain staffings, such as the development of an initial case plan, a case plan in which the goal will be changed to adoption, or when another major change is planned.

C-3. Court Preparation.

    6. Develop a case theory and strategy to follow at hearings and negotiations.

Action

At the beginning of the case, the agency attorney should try to project the future of the case and think through the steps that the caseworker and attorney will need to take to ensure the desired outcomes. In establishing the case theory and strategy, the agency attorney should think about concurrent planning, planning for reunification for the child as well as other permanency outcomes if needed. The legal steps the agency attorney takes at the beginning of a case lay the groundwork for strong case planning by the agency and positive outcomes for the child and family throughout the life of the case. The case theory and strategy should have some flexibility built in so that as the agency attorney receives additional facts and information, the theory and strategy can be amended.

Commentary

Each case has its own facts, and more importantly, concerns an individual child and family. The agency attorney should give each case his or her full attention. By creating a case theory and strategy, the attorney will ensure that he or she analyzes the case thoroughly and thinks through its intricacies to increase the chance that the agency will be well represented and the result will be the best possible outcome for the child.

7. Prepare or help prepare the initial petition and all subsequent pleadings.

Action

The agency attorney should play a lead role in drafting a petition or at least editing and/or reviewing a draft before a petition is filed with court. Similarly, the attorney should review the affidavit and supporting documentation before filing.

Commentary

The initial petition, as well as later petitions, are influential legal documents. The petition controls admissibility of evidence and has a strong impact on the judge and other parties. In general, caseworkers are not trained to write legal documents. If the agency attorney does not draft the petition, or at least review and edit a petition that a caseworker drafts, the agency may miss an important opportunity to shape its case and lay a legal foundation. A legal assistant who works for the agency attorney may be the appropriate person to prepare initial drafts of petitions when attorneys are unable to do so. If the lawyer or legal assistant does draft the petition, it should be based on information the caseworker provides.

8. Timely file all pleadings, motions, and briefs.

Action
The attorney must file petitions (including termination of parental rights petitions), motions, requests for discovery, and responses and answers to pleadings filed by other parties. These pleadings must be thorough, accurate and timely.

Commentary
The agency is generally the moving party in abuse and neglect proceedings. The motions and pleadings the agency attorney files frame the case and must, therefore, be complete and contain all relevant information.

9. Obtain all documents and information needed, including copies of all pleadings and relevant notices filed by other parties.

Action
The agency attorney must ensure all relevant information is brought to the court's attention. To do so, the attorney should request notes and documents, when needed, from the caseworker. Further, the agency attorney should counsel the caseworker to make sure he or she obtains records that are needed, or may be needed for later hearings. For example, the casework file should include full mental health and substance abuse treatment records, histories for the children and parents, abuse and neglect reports with supporting materials about the investigation, education records, health records, birth certificates for the children, death certificates, affidavits of efforts to locate parents, and results of paternity tests. If the caseworker cannot obtain the necessary documents, the attorney may need to personally obtain them or request a court order so the agency may obtain what might otherwise be confidential documents.

Commentary
Strong exhibits and documentary evidence can make or break a case. Knowing what the documents contain is essential to fully prepare a case. Therefore, the agency attorney should ensure all necessary documents are available for preparation and court.

10. Participate in all depositions, negotiations, discovery, pretrial conferences, mediation sessions (when appropriate), and hearings.

Commentary
Jurisdictions vary concerning pre-hearing activity. A great deal of information can be shared during the pre-trial stage of a case, and may help

reduce conflict, and save court time and resources. Therefore, the agency attorney should be actively involved in this stage.

11. Participate in settlement negotiations and attempt speedy resolution of the case, when appropriate.

Action
The agency attorney should participate in settlement negotiations to promptly resolve the case, keeping in mind the effect of continuances and delays on the child. Agency attorneys should be trained in negotiation skills and be comfortable resolving cases outside a courtroom setting. However, the attorney must keep the agency's position in mind while negotiating. Certain things cannot be compromised (e.g., the child's safety, the key underlying facts of the case, or the assignment of culpability in abuse cases) and all parties should be aware of them. The attorney must communicate all settlement offers to the agency, and it is the agency's decision whether to settle. The attorney must be willing to try the case and not compromise on every point to avoid the hearing. The attorney should use mediation resources when available.

Commentary
Negotiation and mediation often result in a detailed agreement among parties of actions that must be taken by all participants. Generally, when agreements have been thoroughly discussed and negotiated all parties feel like they had a say in the decision and are, therefore, more willing to adhere to a plan. Negotiated settlements generally happen quicker than full hearings and therefore move a case along in a reasonable time period. The agency attorney should ensure that the court is notified of the settlement so it can adjust its calendar accordingly.

12. Develop a case timeline and tickler system.

Action
At the beginning of a case, the agency attorney and caseworker should develop timelines that specify what actions should be taken and when. The attorney should keep federal and state laws in mind. For example, under the Adoption and Safe Families Act, the attorney will need to ensure that a permanency hearing occurs at 12 months and will need to file a termination of parental rights petition when the child has been in care for 15 of 22 months, unless certain exceptions apply. The attorney should know when the 15-month point is and whether any exceptions apply. If exceptions apply, the attorney should have a tickler system to revisit whether the exceptions continue to apply at future permanency hearings. Additionally, the agency attorney should develop a tickler system or a plan for remembering the timelines.

Commentary
Agency attorneys handle many cases at a time and must be organized to juggle them all. A good calendaring system, implemented at the beginning and used throughout each case, can help the attorneys better manage their cases. The agency attorney shares a responsibility with the agency for keeping deadlines in mind and moving a case forward.

13. Subpoena and prepare all witnesses, including the client.

Action
The agency attorney should develop a witness list well before a hearing. The attorney should, when possible, call the potential witness to determine whether the witness can provide helpful testimony, and then, when appropriate, let them know a subpoena is on its way. The attorney should also ensure the subpoena is served. Attorneys should set aside time to prepare all witnesses in person before the hearing. Some witnesses may require written questions. These should be provided when needed. Additionally, the agency attorney should counsel the agency on its obligations when agency staff are served with subpoenas by opposing parties.

Commentary
Preparation is the key to successfully resolving a case, either in negotiation or trial. The attorney should plan as early as possible for the case and make arrangements accordingly. The agency attorney should consider working with other parties who share the agency's position (such as the child's representative) when creating a witness list, issuing subpoenas, and preparing witnesses. Doctors, nurses, teachers, therapists, and other potential witnesses have busy schedules and need advance warning about the date and time of the hearing. The agency attorney should do whatever possible to minimize the time a witness must spend in court, such as requesting a time-certain hearing or arranging for the witness to testify on speakerphone from his or her office. Witnesses are often nervous about testifying in court. Attorneys should prepare them thoroughly so they feel comfortable with the process and the questions they will likely be asked. The agency attorney should know what the witness will say on the stand.

14. Ensure proper notice is provided to all parties and necessary caretakers.

Action
The agency attorney should either send proper notice to parties and caretakers from the attorney office, or ensure that it is being done by the agency or court.

Commentary
ASFA requires that foster parents and relative caretakers receive notice of all review and permanency hearings. Parties to the case must receive notice of court hearings and motions filed with the court, such as TPR petitions. As the moving party in most proceedings, the agency has a duty to ensure this requirement is implemented properly. Since it is a legal obligation, the agency attorney should be directly involved. The agency attorney should ensure whoever is providing the notice provides it to noncustodial parents and any man who may have paternity rights to the child.

C-4. Hearings.

15. Attend and prepare for all hearings.

Action
The agency attorney should attend and prepare for all hearings and participate in all telephone or other conferences with the court.

Commentary
If the agency is to be well represented, the agency attorney must be prepared and present in court. Even in jurisdictions in which the agency attorney represents the state, the attorney must be active in all stages of the court process to protect children and ensure their safety. In some jurisdictions a nonattorney representative from the agency appears in court on uncontested matters. In such a jurisdiction, there should be a system in place for a caseworker to request legal assistance before court, and an attorney should be available if the case becomes complicated. Even if the agency attorney has taken these precautions, it is possible that an unauthorized practice of law issue may arise from this practice.

16. Prepare and make all appropriate motions and evidentiary objections.

Action
The agency attorney should make appropriate motions and evidentiary objections to advance the agency's position during the hearing. If necessary, the agency attorney should file briefs in support of the agency's position on evidentiary issues. The agency attorney should preserve legal issues for appeal.

Commentary
It is essential that agency attorneys understand the state's Rules of Evidence and all court rules and procedures. While there are many circumstances in which cases settle through alternative dispute resolution

or during the pretrial phase of the case, agency attorneys must be comfortable zealously trying a case in court. To do so, the attorney must be willing and able to make appropriate motions, objections, and arguments.

17. Present case-in-chief, present and cross-examine witnesses, prepare and present exhibits.

Action

The attorney must be able to coherently present witnesses to move his or her case forward. The witness must be prepared in advance and the attorney should know what evidence he or she expects to present through the witness. The attorney must also be skilled at cross-examining opposing parties' witnesses in an effective, but nonmalicious, manner. The attorney must know how to offer documents, photos and physical objects into evidence.

Commentary

Because the agency is generally the moving party in most hearings, the burden is on the agency attorney to present a solid case with well-prepared witnesses and documentary evidence. The agency attorney must ensure that appropriate witnesses, e.g., caseworkers who are familiar with the entire case, are present in court and prepared to testify. Additionally, it is important that the agency attorney is comfortable cross-examining witnesses when the other parties present their cases.

18. In jurisdictions in which a jury trial is possible, participate in jury selection and drafting jury instructions.

Commentary

Several jurisdictions around the country afford parties in child welfare cases the right to a jury trial at the adjudicatory or termination of parental rights stages. Agency attorneys in those jurisdictions should be skilled at choosing an appropriate jury, drafting jury instructions that are favorable to the agency's position, and trying the case before individuals who may not be familiar with child abuse and neglect issues.

19. Request the opportunity to make brief opening and closing arguments when appropriate.

Action

When permitted by the judge, the agency attorney should make opening and closing arguments in the case to set the scene and ensure the judge understands the issues.

Commentary

In many child abuse and neglect proceedings, attorneys do not make opening and closing arguments. However, these arguments can help shape the way the judge views the case and therefore can help the attorney. Argument may be especially needed, for example, in complicated cases when information from expert witnesses should be highlighted for the judge, in hearings that take place over a number of days, or when there are several children and the agency is requesting different things for each of them.

20. Prepare or help prepare proposed findings of fact, conclusions of law, and orders when they will be used in the court's decision.

Action

Proposed findings of fact, conclusions of law, and orders can be prepared before a hearing. When the judge is prepared to enter his or her ruling, the judge can use the proposed findings or amend them as appropriate. Once the order is made, the agency attorney should ensure a written order is entered and provided to the agency.

Commentary

By preparing the proposed findings of fact and conclusions of law, the agency attorney has the opportunity to frame the case and ruling for the judge. This may assure accurate orders are entered that meet federally mandated requirements, such as reasonable efforts findings. It may also result in orders that favor the agency, preserve appellate issues, and help the agency attorney clarify desired outcomes before a hearing begins. The agency attorney could provide the judge with the proposed findings and orders on a computer disk or electronically when the judge requests. When a judge prefers not to receive these proposed findings and orders, the agency attorney should not be required to provide them.

C-5. Post Hearings/Appeals.

21. Follow all court orders pertaining to the attorney for the client/agency.

Commentary

There may be times the judge orders an agency attorney to do something, such as file a termination of parental rights petition by a certain date. The agency attorney must comply with such orders, or appeal them as appropriate.

22. Review court orders to ensure accuracy and clarity and review with agency when necessary.

Action
After the hearing, the agency attorney and caseworker should each review the written order to ensure it reflects the court's verbal order. If the order is incorrect, the attorney should take whatever steps are necessary to correct it. If the order is correct but controversial, the caseworker is unhappy with it, or the caseworker has trouble understanding what is required, the agency attorney should review it with the caseworker and/or the caseworker's supervisor and potentially the agency's administrator and the attorney's supervisor. Follow whatever conflict resolution system is developed (see D-1). The agency attorney should counsel the agency to follow the order until a stay or other relief is secured.

23. Take reasonable steps to ensure the agency complies with court orders.

Action
The agency attorney should monitor the agency's efforts to implement the order and answer any questions the caseworker may have about the agency's obligations under the order.

Commentary
Obligations 22 and 23 illustrate the importance of the agency attorney's role outside the courtroom. The attorney should help the agency understand and follow through with the court's orders to protect the agency, but more importantly to ensure the agency provides the best possible services for children and families as ordered by the court.

24. Consider and discuss with the agency the possibility of appeal.

Action
The agency attorney should consider and discuss with the agency caseworker and supervisor the possibility of appeal when a court's ruling is contrary to the agency's position or interests. The decision to appeal should be a joint one between the attorney and agency staff and must have an appropriate legal basis.

Commentary
When discussing the possibility of an appeal, the attorney should explain both the positive and negative effects of an appeal, including the impact the appeal could have on the child's best interests. For instance, if a judge made a poor decision that could negatively

impact the child's future and his or her chance at permanency, an appeal should be taken. Conversely, an appeal might unnecessarily delay a case or make "bad law" for future cases in which the agency participates. The agency attorney should not decide against an appeal because of concern about the trial judge's reaction. *See* section E-2, 10 for a discussion of appellate strategy.

25. If a decision is made to appeal, timely file the necessary post-hearing motions and the notice to appeal paperwork.

Action
The agency attorney should carefully review his or her obligations in the state's Rules of Appellate Procedure. The attorney should timely file all paperwork, including requests for stays of the trial court order, transcript and case file. The appellate brief should be clear, concise and comprehensive and also timely filed. If arguments are scheduled, the attorney should be prepared, organized and direct. In jurisdictions in which a different attorney than the trial attorney handles the appeal, the agency attorney should identify issues that are appropriate for appeal and work with the new attorney on the appeal. As the attorney who handled the trial, the agency attorney may have insight beyond what the new attorney could get by reading the trial transcript.

Commentary
Appellate skills differ from the skills most agency attorneys use day-to-day. The agency attorney may wish to seek guidance from an experienced appellate advocate when drafting the brief and preparing for argument. An appeal can have a great deal of impact on the trial judge who heard the case and in trial courts throughout the state.

26. Request an expedited appeal, when feasible, and file all necessary paperwork while the appeal is pending.

Action
If the state court allows, the attorney should always request an expedited appeal. In this request, the attorney should provide information about why the case should be expedited such as any special characteristics about the child and why delay would be personally harmful to this child. The request for an expedited appeal should always be considered.

Commentary
Appeals can delay the court process. Every effort should be made to move the child's case forward. The attorney should take great care during the appellate process to do so.

27. Communicate the results of the appeal and its implications to the client/agency.

Action

The agency attorney should communicate the result and its implications to the agency. If, as a result of the appeal, the agency needs to take action in the case, it should be instructed to do so. If, as a result of the appeal, the attorney needs to file any motions with the trial court, the attorney should do so.

D. Ethical and Practice Considerations

D-1. Ensure a conflict resolution system is created.

Action

The agency attorney and agency should jointly develop a conflict resolution system to cover attorney-caseworker conflict and conflicts among caseworkers.[9]

Key principles of the system should include: 1) the attorney and caseworker (or two caseworkers) should start with a face-to-face meeting to try to resolve the conflict; 2) if there is no resolution, the system should delineate how each should go up their respective chains of command; and 3) the system should set out examples of issues that are legal and those that are social work decisions, understanding that most issues will need to be resolved jointly. The system should incorporate timeframes for resolution so as not to delay a case. The agency attorney should prepare a caseworker before court so that conflicts do not surface in front of the judge.

Commentary

A conflict resolution system should be in place before conflict occurs. The attorneys and caseworkers should work as a team to reach the best outcomes for children and families.

D-2. Understand and comply with state and federal privacy and confidentiality laws.

Action

The agency attorney must understand and comply with state and federal privacy and confidentiality laws, including releases of information and protective orders. The agency attorney should also develop protocols with the agency to help the agency access confidential information from external sources when needed for the case. Such methods might include obtaining court orders to access the necessary information.

Commentary
Because the child welfare system directly impacts the lives of children and families, there are numerous aspects of the system that are regulated by confidentiality laws and procedures. For example, the identity of the child, parents, and reporters, as well as treatment records and HIV status of any of the parties, must all be kept confidential. Additionally, the agency attorney should be aware of any HIPPA (medical records) or FERPA (education records) issues that arise. The agency attorney should thoroughly understand these laws to help the agency develop procedures, for example, concerning redacting confidential information from case files for discovery, and following them.

D-3. Initiate and maintain positive working relationships with other professionals in the child welfare system.

Action
Because of the crucial role the agency attorney plays in the child welfare system, he or she should build relationships with the other professionals in the system. These include, but are not limited to:

- Judges
- Court staff
- Opposing counsel
- Child advocates, both attorney and nonattorney
- Criminal prosecutors
- CASAs
- Child Advocacy Centers
- Multidisciplinary Teams/Child Fatality Review Teams
- Key service providers
- Medical and mental health professionals
- School staff
- Other local child-centered organizations

Commentary
Maintaining positive relationships with other professionals will benefit the agency on individual cases as well as during times of reform. When these community members believe their opinion is valued and they are an integral part of the child welfare system as a whole, they will lend their support in different ways, such as when the agency seeks legislative support or buy-in for new projects.

D-4. Play an active role in deciding whether the child should testify and/or be present in the courtroom during hearings.

Action

The agency attorney should consult with the caseworker and the child's attorney or GAL to decide whether the child should be present and/ or testify at a hearing. It is important to consider the child's wishes, any possible effects of the testimony and the child's developmental ability to handle cross-examination. The agency attorney and child's attorney should decide together who will present the child's testimony. If the child is represented by an attorney (including an attorney serving as a guardian ad litem), the agency attorney may not speak with the child directly without the permission of the child's attorney, because the child is not his or her client.[10] Questions posed to the child should be clear and asked with the child's ability to understand in mind.[11] Consider requesting an *in camera* hearing, excluding the parents from the courtroom, or videotape for the child's testimony.

Even when the child is not testifying, there may be a benefit to having the child present in court.[12] For example, the child's presence may help the judge focus specifically on the child's needs, and the child may understand how the court makes its decisions. The basis of the decision concerning the child's presence in court should be any state law concerning the child's right to be in court and the child's safety, best interests, and emotional well-being. The agency attorney and caseworker, in coordination with the child's attorney or GAL, should consider whether being in court will be helpful to the child, whether he or she may want to be a part of the proceedings, and whether the child's presence will advance the position of the agency.

Commentary

Generally, the child should be present at substantive hearings because the proceeding concerns the child's life and the child's input must be considered. If the child can handle being in court, his or her presence is important because the judge and other parties should have the opportunity to become acquainted with the child as an individual.[13] This may have an important tactical impact on the case. For example, it is more difficult to continue a case when the judge actually sees the child getting bigger and older and remaining in foster care with no status change. However, if the child will be traumatized by the experience, he or she should not be present in court.

Deciding whether to call the child as a witness can be difficult. There could be a conflict between the caseworker's judgment and the agency attorney's recommendation on strategy to win a case. For example, in a sexual abuse case, the caseworker may believe it would be too difficult for the child to testify, whereas the attorney may think that without the child's testimony the judge would dismiss the case. In this type of situation, the attorney and caseworker should resolve the issue before court and may need to use the conflict resolution system as set forth in D-1 above. If the child is called to testify during the agency's case in chief, opposing parties and the judge may agree to allow the child's attorney to conduct the direct examination to make the child more comfortable. The judge may also agree to hear the child in chambers so the child does not have to testify in front of the parents. In a civil action there is no absolute right to confrontation and if the parents' attorneys are present to hear the child's testimony, generally the parents' rights are considered to be protected.

E. Administrative Responsibilities

E-1. Obligations of Agency Attorney Managers.[14]

1. Clarify attorney roles and expectations;
2. Determine and set reasonable caseloads for agency attorneys;
3. Develop a system for the continuity of representation;
4. Provide agency attorneys with training and education opportunities;
5. Create a brief and forms bank;
6. Ensure the office has quality technical and support staff;
7. Develop and follow a hiring practice focused on hiring highly qualified candidates;
8. Develop and implement an attorney evaluation process;
9. Advocate for competitive salaries for staff attorneys;
10. Act as advisor, counselor and trainer for the agency;
11. Work actively with external entities to improve the child welfare system.

Commentary
In general, this section applies to attorneys in an organized office setting, not one attorney government law office or solo practitioners.

E-2. Fulfilling Agency Attorney Manager Obligations.

1. Clarify attorney roles and expectations.

Action
The agency attorney manager, with the agency administration, should clearly set expectations for the agency attorneys. This may include:

- written job descriptions;
- responsibilities concerning work with the caseworkers; and
- protocols for assigning tasks and delineating timeframes.[15]

The agency attorney manager should ensure the agency attorneys perform their required tasks and ensure the agency understands and performs its roles.

Commentary

For agency attorneys to provide the best possible representation, both the attorneys and agency must understand their roles and responsibilities. There should be a collaborative approach. The agency attorney manager plays a key role in fostering this teamwork and clarifying each participant's obligations.

2. Determine and set reasonable caseloads for agency attorneys.[16]

Action

An agency attorney manager should determine reasonable caseload levels for the agency attorneys and then monitor the attorneys to ensure the maximum is not exceeded. Consider a caseload/workload study, review written materials about such studies, or look into caseload sizes in similar counties to accurately determine the ideal caseload for attorneys in the office. Be sure to have a consistent definition of what a "case" is – a family or a child. When assessing the appropriate number of cases, remember to account for all agency attorney obligations, case difficulty, the time required to thoroughly prepare a case, support staff assistance, travel time, level of experience of attorneys, and available time (excluding vacation, holidays, sick leave, training and other non-case-related activity). If the agency attorney manager carries a caseload, the number of cases should reflect the time the individual spends on management duties.

Commentary

High caseload is considered one of the major barriers to quality representation and a source of high attorney turnover. It is essential to decide what a reasonable caseload is in your jurisdiction. How attorneys define cases and attorney obligations vary from place-to-place, but having a manageable caseload is crucial. One study found that a caseload of 40–50 active cases is reasonable, and a caseload of over 60 cases is unmanageable.[17] The standards drafting committee recommended a caseload of no more than 60.

3. Develop a system for the continuity of representation.

Action

The agency attorney manager should develop a case assignment system that fosters ownership and involvement in the case by the agency attorney. The office can have a one-attorney: one-case (vertical representation) policy in which an attorney follows the case from initial filing through permanency and handles all aspects of the case. Alternatively, the cases may be assigned to a group of attorneys who handle all aspects of a case as a team and are all assigned to one judge or one group of caseworkers.

Commentary
Agency attorneys can provide the best representation for the agency, and therefore get the best results for children, when they know a case and are invested in its outcome. Additionally, having attorneys who are assigned to particular cases decreases delays because the attorney does not need to learn the case each time it is scheduled for court. Rather, the attorney has the opportunity to monitor action on the case between court hearings. This system also makes it easier for the agency attorney manager to track how cases are handled.

> ## 4. Provide agency attorneys with training and education opportunities.

Action
The agency attorney manager must ensure that each agency attorney has the opportunity to participate in training and education programs. When a new agency attorney is hired, the agency attorney manager should assess that attorney's level of experience and readiness to handle cases. The agency attorney manager should develop an internal training program during which the new attorney will be paired with an experienced "attorney mentor" who will work with the new attorney. The new attorney should be required to: 1) observe each type of court proceeding (and mediation if available in the jurisdiction), 2) second-chair each type of proceeding, 3) try each type of case with the mentor second-chairing, and 4) try each type of proceeding on his or her own, with the mentor available to assist, before the attorney can begin handling cases alone.

Additionally, each attorney should be required to attend [fill in number of hours, at least 12] hours of training before beginning, and [at least 10 hours] of training every year after. Training should include general legal topics such as evidence and trial skills, and child welfare-specific topics, such as:

- Relevant State, Federal and Case Law, Procedures and Rules
- Agency Policies and Procedures
- Available Community Resources

- Legal Permanency Options
- Termination of Parental Rights Law
- Adoption Subsidies
- Child Development
- Child-Centered Communication
- Legal Ethics as it Relates to Agency Representation
- Negotiation Strategies and Techniques
- How Domestic Violence Impacts Children in the Child Welfare System
- Appellate Advocacy
- Immigration Law as it Relates to Child Welfare Cases
- Education Law as it Relates to Child Welfare Cases
- State and Federal Benefit Programs Affecting Children in Foster Care (e.g., SSI, SSA, Medicaid)
- Understanding Mental Illness
- Issues Arising from Substance Abuse
- Understanding the Impact of Out-of-Home Placement on Children
- Basic Principles of Attachment Theory
- Options for Presenting Children's Testimony
- Sexual Abuse
- Dynamics of Physical Abuse and Neglect and How To Prove It
  - Shaken Baby Syndrome
  - Broken Bones
  - Burns
  - Failure to Thrive

Commentary
Agency attorneys should be encouraged to learn as much as possible and participate in conferences and trainings to expand their understanding of developments in the child welfare field. While agency attorneys are often overworked and do not have extra time to attend conferences, the knowledge they gain will be invaluable. The philosophy of the office should stress the need for ongoing learning and professional growth. The agency attorney manager should require the attorneys to attend an achievable number of hours of training that will match the training needs of the attorneys. The agency, court and Court Improvement Program[18] may have training money available that the agency attorney manager may be able to access to defray costs of agency attorney training. Similarly, the agency attorney manager should reach out to the state and local bar associations, area law schools or local Child Law Institutes to learn about available education

opportunities. Further, the agency attorney manager should ensure the attorneys have access to professional publications to stay current on the law and promising practices in child welfare.

5. Create a brief and forms bank.

Action
Develop standard briefs, memoranda of law and forms that attorneys can use, so they do not "reinvent the wheel" for each new project. For example, there could be sample discovery request forms, motions, notice of appeal, and even petitions. Similarly, memoranda of law and appellate briefs follow certain patterns that the attorney could copy and only have to fill in the specific facts of a case. These forms and briefs should be available on the computer and hard copy and should be maintained in a central location.

6. Ensure the office has quality technical and support staff.

Action
The agency attorney manager should advocate for high quality technical and staff support. The agency attorney must have adequate and operational equipment to do the high-level job described in these standards. Additionally, quality staff support is essential. The office should employ qualified legal assistants and administrative assistants to help the agency attorney. The agency attorney manager should create detailed job descriptions for these staff members to be sure they are providing necessary assistance. For instance, a qualified legal assistant can do research, help draft petitions, schedule and help prepare witnesses and more.

Commentary
The agency attorney cannot do a good job when he or she spends a lot of time trying to get the copy machine to work. The attorney must at least have access to a good quality computer, voice mail, fax machine and copier to get the work done efficiently and with as little stress as possible. Also, by employing qualified staff, the attorney will be free to perform tasks essential to quality representation.

7. Develop and follow a hiring practice focused on hiring highly qualified candidates.

Action
The agency attorney manager should give a great deal of attention to hiring the best attorney possible. The agency attorney manager should form a hiring committee made up of managing and line agency

attorneys and possibly an agency representative. Desired qualities of a new agency attorney should be determined, focusing on educational and professional achievements; experience and commitment to the child welfare field; interpersonal skills; diversity and the needs of the office; writing and verbal skills; and ability to handle pressure. Advertising the position widely will help draw in a wider group of candidates. The hiring committee should set clear criteria for screening candidates before interviews and should then conduct thorough interviews and post-interview discussions to choose the candidate with the best skills and strongest commitment. Reference checks should be done before making an offer.[19]

Commentary
Hiring high quality attorneys is essential to raising the level of representation and the level of services the agency receives. The agency attorney job is difficult. There are many tasks to complete in a short time. Since the agency attorneys often move the rest of the system, strong, committed attorneys can drastically improve the system.

8. Develop and implement an attorney evaluation process.

Action
The agency attorney manager should develop an evaluation system that focuses on consistency, constructive criticism, and improvement. Some factors to evaluate include: moving cases to permanency in a timely manner; preparation and trial skills; ability to work with agency and other professionals; and ability to work as a team player. During the evaluation process, the agency attorney manager should consider observing the attorney in court, reviewing the attorney's files, talking with colleagues and agency representatives about the attorney's performance, having the attorney fill out a self evaluation, and meeting in person with the attorney. The evaluation should be based on information, which the agency attorney manager will need to collect.[20]

Commentary
A solid attorney evaluation process helps attorneys know what they should be working on, what management believes are priorities, what they are doing well and where they need improvement. If a positive process is created, the attorneys will feel supported in their positions and empowered to improve.

9. Advocate for competitive salaries for staff attorneys.

Action

Agency attorney managers should advocate for salaries for the agency attorneys that are competitive with other government attorneys in the jurisdiction. To recruit and retain experienced attorneys, salaries must compare favorably with similarly situated attorneys.

Commentary

While resources are scarce, agency attorneys deserve to be paid a competitive wage. They will not be able to stay in their position nor be motivated to work harder without a reasonable salary. High attorney turnover may decrease when attorneys are paid well.

10. Act as advisor, counselor, and trainer for the agency.[21]

Action

The agency attorney manager must ensure that the agency is receiving high quality representation both inside and outside the courtroom. No matter what model of representation, agency attorneys should be sure agency staff is fully informed about legal matters and fully prepared for court and policy decisions. The agency attorney manager should, therefore, develop protocols concerning such issues as:

- communication, such as regular office hours at the agency and timely responses by attorneys to agency telephone calls and emails;
- information sharing;
- conflict resolution;
- attorney-client work product and confidentiality issues; and
- dealing with media and high-profile cases.

The agency attorney manager should be sure there is a system in place for reviewing all court orders and communicating the results with the agency.

The agency attorney manager should work with the agency to develop an overall strategy for appeals. It should identify the list of issues that will be most important and appropriate to appeal. It should include an internal system for bringing potential appeals to the agency attorneys and agency attorney manager's attention. The agency attorney manager should then be ready to pursue the strategy when appropriate cases arise.

The agency attorney manager should help prepare all federal reviews and implement any program improvement plans that result.

The agency attorney manager should ensure there is a process for agency legal training. As part of the process, the agency attorney manager could design materials, with samples, to help caseworkers prepare for court and provide testimony. Agency training could occur during formal, new hire training, at brown bag lunches or during after-hours courses. Topics could include, for example:

- overviews of state and federal laws;
- writing appropriate court reports and case plans;
- testifying in court;
- the trial and appellate court processes; and
- the need for and steps to complete acceptable searches for absent parents.

Commentary
Regardless of whether the agency attorney represents the agency or the state, the caseworkers often have the information needed to put together a strong case. Therefore, the attorneys and caseworkers must meet and communicate regularly. This could involve having office hours when the caseworkers can visit and ask questions or designating an attorney to take caseworkers' telephone calls. Similarly, the better the caseworkers and agency staff understand the law and legal process, the easier it is for them and the agency attorneys to do their jobs well. The agency attorney manager should be responsible for developing a system for training the agency staff as well as protocols to improve the working relationships between the agency and agency attorneys.

11. Work actively with external entities to improve the child welfare system.

Action
The agency attorney manager should act as a liaison between the agency and outside entities involved in the child welfare system. For example, the agency attorney manager should meet regularly with the court and the state Court Improvement Program to improve issues concerning court administration. The agency attorney manager (or designee) should sit on all multidisciplinary committees charged with improving court functions or other aspects of the system. The agency attorney manager should be in regular contact with agencies, such as local hospitals or schools, that employ people who are frequently called as witnesses and who do work with the same population of children. Doing so can build strong relationships and improve the care the children receive from all of the involved agencies. The agency attorney manager should reach out to agencies such as law enforcement and

treatment facilities that have information or documents often needed for litigation.

Commentary

The agency attorney manager should be visible in the community and provide a positive face for people to associate with the agency and agency attorney's office. The agency attorney manager should understand the many issues the agency faces and help resolve some of these through work with the court and other involved entities.

ACKNOWLEDGMENTS

These standards were drafted by Mimi Laver, Legal Education Director, ABA Center on Children and the Law, with the help of a committee. Many thanks to all of them for their time, expertise, and assistance in making these standards useful and practice focused. These members are:

Diane Bennett, Lead Deputy County Counsel, Santa Clara County, California

Bruce Boyer, Director and Clinical Professor Loyola University Chicago, and Chair, ABA Standing Committee on the Unmet Legal Needs of Children

Diane Garrity, Partner, Serra, Garrity & Masiowski, LLC and former General Counsel, New Mexico Children, Youth and Families Department

Marguerite Gualtieri, Child Advocate Staff Attorney Support Center for Child Advocates, and Co-chair of the ABA Section of Litigation Children's Rights Litigation Committee.

Connie Hickman Tanner, Director of Juvenile Courts, Arkansas

Virginia Peel, General Counsel Massachusetts Department of Social Services

Marvin Ventrell, Executive Director, National Association of Counsel for Children

Howard Davidson, Director, ABA Center on Children and the Law

Mark Hardin, Director of Child Welfare, ABA Center on Children and the Law

Cecilia Fiermonte, Assistant Director, ABA Center on Children and the Law

Kathleen McNaught, Assistant Director, ABA Center on Children and the Law

Moreen Murphy, Staff Director, ABA Standing Committee on the Unmet Legal Needs of Children

Thanks also to:

Jennifer Renne, Assistant Director, ABA Center on Children and the Law, for her expertise and assistance on issues involving ethics and the ABA Model Rules of Professional Conduct and

Claire Sandt, Editor, ABA Center on Children and the Law, for her help in making these standards more clear and organized.

NOTES

1. Model Rules of Prof'l Conduct R. 1.13 (Organization as Client).
2. Model Rule 1.13 (Organization as Client).
3. Model Rule 1.13 (Organization as Client), cmt. 9&10.
4. Renne, Jennifer. "Handling Conflicts of Interest in Child Welfare Cases." *Child Law Practice*, June 2004.
5. Model Rule 1.1 (Competence).
6. Model Rule 1.4 (Communication).
7. Model Rule 2.1 (Advisor).
8. Model Rule 1.3 (Diligence).
9. Model Rules 1.2 (Scope of Representation) and 1.13, cmt, 3.
10. Model Rule 4.2 (Communication with Person Represented by Counsel).
11. *American Bar Association Standards of Practice for Lawyers Who Represent Children in Abuse and Neglect Case.* D-5–D-9. Washington, DC: 1996.
12. NACC Recommendations for Representation of Children in Abuse and Neglect Cases. III A 6. Denver, CO: National Association of Counsel for Children, 2001.
13. *Id.*
14. Model Rule 5.1 (Responsibility of Partners, Managers and Supervisory Lawyers).
15. Laver, Mimi. Chapter 8, "Agency Attorneys and Caseworkers: Working Well Together," *Foundations for Success Strengthening Your Agency Attorney Office.* Washington, DC: American Bar Association, 1999.
16. Model Rules 1.1 (Competence) and 1.3 (Diligence).
17. Segal, Ellen. *Evaluating and Improving Child Welfare Agency Legal Representation: Self Assessment Instrument and Commentary.* Washington, D.C.: ABA National Legal Resource Center for Child Advocacy and Protection, 1990, 17.
18. The Court Improvement Program (CIP) is a federal grant to each state's (as well as the District of Columbia and Puerto Rico) supreme court. The funds must be used to improve child abuse and neglect courts. States vary in how they allocate the dollars, but it typically involves training, benchbooks, pilot projects, model courts and information technology systems for the courts.
19. Laver, Mimi. Chapter 2, "So You're Hiring? A Guide to Choosing the Best Candidate," *Foundations for Success Strengthening Your Agency Attorney Office.* Washington, DC: American Bar Association, 1999.
20. Laver, Mimi. Chapter 4, "Getting the Most from Performance Evaluations," *Foundations for Success Strengthening Your Agency Attorney Office.* Washington, DC: American Bar Association, 1999.
21. Model Rule 2.1 (Advisor).

Standards of Practice for Attorneys Representing Parents in Abuse and Neglect Cases

AUGUST 2006

INTRODUCTION

These standards promote quality representation and uniformity of practice throughout the country for parents' attorneys in child abuse and neglect cases. The standards were written with the help of a committee of practicing parents' attorneys and child welfare professionals from different jurisdictions in the country. With their help, the standards were written with the difficulties of day-to-day practice in mind, but also with the goal of raising the quality of representation. While local adjustments may be necessary to apply these standards in practice, jurisdictions should strive to meet their fundamental principles and spirit.

The standards are divided into the following categories:

1. Summary of the Standards
2. Basic Obligations of Parents' Attorneys
3. Obligations of Attorney Manager
4. The Role of the Court

The standards include "black letter" requirements written in bold. Following the black letter standards are "actions." These actions further discuss how to fulfill the standard; implementing each standard requires the accompanying action. After the action is "commentary" or a discussion of why the standard is necessary and how it should be applied. When a standard does not need further explanation, no action or commentary appears. Several standards relate to specific sections of the Model Rules of Professional Conduct, and the Model Rules are referenced in these standards. The terms "parent" and "client" are used interchangeably throughout the document. These standards apply to all attorneys who represent parents in child abuse and neglect cases, whether they work for an agency or privately.

As was done in the *Standards of Practice for Attorneys Representing Child Welfare Agencies*, ABA 2004, a group of standards for attorney managers is included in these standards. These standards primarily apply to parents' attorneys who work for an agency or law firm – an institutional model of representation. Solo practitioners, or attorneys who individually receive appointments from the court, may wish to review this part of the standards, but may find some do not apply. However, some standards in this section, such as those about training and caseload, are relevant for all parents' attorneys.

As was done in the *Standards of Practice for Lawyers Who Represent Children in Abuse and Neglect Cases*, ABA 1996, a section of the standards concerns the Role of the Court in implementing these *Standards*. The ABA and the National Council of Juvenile and Family Court Judges have policies concerning the importance of the court in ensuring that all parties in abuse and neglect cases have competent representation.

Representing a parent in an abuse and neglect case is a difficult and emotional job. There are many responsibilities. These standards are intended to help the attorney prioritize duties and manage the practice in a way that will benefit each parent on the attorney's caseload.

SUMMARY: ABA STANDARDS OF PRACTICE FOR ATTORNEYS REPRESENTING PARENTS IN ABUSE AND NEGLECT CASES

Basic Obligations
The parent's attorney shall:

General:

1. Adhere to all relevant jurisdiction-specific training and mentoring requirements before accepting a court appointment to represent a parent in an abuse or neglect case.

2. Acquire sufficient working knowledge of all relevant federal and state laws, regulations, policies, and rules.
3. Understand and protect the parent's rights to information and decision making while the child is in foster care.
4. Actively represent a parent in the pre-petition phase of a case, if permitted within the jurisdiction.
5. Avoid continuances (or reduce empty adjournments) and work to reduce delays in court proceedings unless there is a strategic benefit for the client.
6. Cooperate and communicate regularly with other professionals in the case.

Relationship with the Client:

7. Advocate for the client's goals and empower the client to direct the representation and make informed decisions based on thorough counsel.
8. Act in accordance with the duty of loyalty owed to the client.
9. Adhere to all laws and ethical obligations concerning confidentiality.
10. Provide the client with contact information in writing and establish a message system that allows regular attorney–client contact.
11. Meet and communicate regularly with the client well before court proceedings. Counsel the client about all legal matters related to the case, including specific allegations against the client, the service plan, the client's rights in the pending proceeding, any orders entered against the client and the potential consequences of failing to obey court orders or cooperate with service plans.
12. Work with the client to develop a case timeline and tickler system.
13. Provide the client with copies of all petitions, court orders, service plans, and other relevant case documents, including reports regarding the child except when expressly prohibited by law, rule or court order.
14. Be alert to and avoid potential conflicts of interest or the appearance of a conflict of interest that would interfere with the competent representation of the client.
15. Act in a culturally competent manner and with regard to the socioeconomic position of the parent throughout all aspects of representation.
16. Take diligent steps to locate and communicate with a missing parent and decide representation strategies based on that communication.

17. Be aware of the unique issues an incarcerated parent faces and provide competent representation to the incarcerated client.

18. Be aware of the client's mental health status and be prepared to assess whether the parent can assist with the case.

Investigation:

19. Conduct a thorough and independent investigation at every stage of the proceeding.

20. Interview the client well before each hearing, in time to use client information for the case investigation.

Informal Discovery:

21. Review the child welfare agency case file.

22. Obtain all necessary documents, including copies of all pleadings and relevant notices filed by other parties, and information from the caseworker and providers.

Formal Discovery:

23. When needed, use formal discovery methods to obtain information.

Court Preparation:

24. Develop a case theory and strategy to follow at hearings and negotiations.
25. Timely file all pleadings, motions, and briefs. Research applicable legal issues and advance legal arguments when appropriate.
26. Engage in case planning and advocate for appropriate social services using a multidisciplinary approach to representation when available.
27. Aggressively advocate for regular visitation in a family-friendly setting.
28. With the client's permission, and when appropriate, engage in settlement negotiations and mediation to resolve the case.
29. Thoroughly prepare the client to testify at the hearing.
30. Identify, locate and prepare all witnesses.
31. Identify, secure, prepare and qualify expert witness when needed. When permissible, interview opposing counsel's experts.

Hearings:

32. Attend and prepare for all hearings, including pretrial conferences.
33. Prepare and make all appropriate motions and evidentiary objections.
34. Present and cross-examine witnesses, prepare and present exhibits.
35. In jurisdictions in which a jury trial is possible, actively participate in jury selection and drafting jury instructions.
36. Request closed proceedings (or a cleared courtroom) in appropriate cases.
37. Request the opportunity to make opening and closing arguments.
38. Prepare proposed findings of fact, conclusions of law and orders when they will be used in the court's decision or may otherwise benefit the client.

Post Hearings/Appeals:

39. Review court orders to ensure accuracy and clarity and review with client.
40. Take reasonable steps to ensure the client complies with court orders and to determine whether the case needs to be brought back to court.
41. Consider and discuss the possibility of appeal with the client.
42. If the client decides to appeal, timely and thoroughly file the necessary post-hearing motions and paperwork related to the appeal and closely follow the jurisdiction's Rules of Appellate Procedure.
43. Request an expedited appeal, when feasible, and file all necessary paperwork while the appeal is pending.
44. Communicate the results of the appeal and its implications to the client.

Obligations of Attorney Managers

Attorney Managers are urged to:

1. Clarify attorney roles and expectations.
2. Determine and set reasonable caseloads for attorneys.
3. Advocate for competitive salaries for staff attorneys.
4. Develop a system for the continuity of representation.

5. Provide attorneys with training and education opportunities regarding the special issues that arise in the client population.
6. Establish a regular supervision schedule.
7. Create a brief and forms bank.
8. Ensure the office has quality technical and support staff as well as adequate equipment, library materials, and computer programs to support its operations.
9. Develop and follow a recruiting and hiring practice focused on hiring highly qualified candidates.
10. Develop and implement an attorney evaluation process.
11. Work actively with other stakeholders to improve the child welfare system, including court procedures.

Role of the Court
The Court is urged to:

1. Recognize the importance of the parent attorney's role.
2. Establish uniform standards of representation for parents' attorneys.
3. Ensure the attorneys who are appointed to represent parents in abuse and neglect cases are qualified, well-trained, and held accountable for practice that complies with these standards.
4. Ensure appointments are made when a case first comes before the court, or before the first hearing, and last until the case has been dismissed from the court's jurisdiction.
5. Ensure parents' attorneys receive fair compensation.
6. Ensure timely payment of fees and costs for attorneys.
7. Provide interpreters, investigators and other specialists needed by the attorneys to competently represent clients. Ensure attorneys are reimbursed for supporting costs, such as use of experts, investigation services, interpreters, etc.
8. Ensure that attorneys who are receiving appointments carry a reasonable caseload that would allow them to provide competent representation for each of their clients.
9. Ensure all parties, including the parent's attorney, receive copies of court orders and other documentation.
10. Provide contact information between clients and attorneys.
11. Ensure child welfare cases are heard promptly with a view towards timely decision making and thorough review of issues.

BASIC OBLIGATIONS

The parent's attorney shall:

General[1]

1. **Adhere to all relevant jurisdiction-specific training and mentoring requirements before accepting a court appointment to represent a parent in an abuse or neglect case.**

Action
The parent's attorney must participate in all required training and mentoring before accepting an appointment.

Commentary
As in all areas of law, it is essential that attorneys learn the substantive law as well as local practice. A parent's fundamental liberty interest in the care and custody of his or her child is at stake, and the attorney must be adequately trained to protect this interest. Because the stakes are so high, the standards drafting committee recommends all parents' attorneys receive a minimum of 20 hours of relevant training before receiving an appointment and a minimum of 15 hours of related training each year. Training should directly relate to the attorney's child welfare practice.[2] This is further detailed in Attorney Managers Standard 5 below. In addition, the parent's attorney should actively participate in ongoing training opportunities. Even if the attorney's jurisdiction does not require training or mentoring, the attorney should seek it. Each state should make comprehensive training available to parents' attorneys throughout the state. Training may include relevant online or video training.

2. **Acquire sufficient working knowledge of all relevant federal and state laws, regulations, policies, and rules.**

Action
Parents' attorneys may come to the practice with competency in the various aspects of child abuse and neglect practice, or they need to be trained on them. It is essential for the parent's attorney to read and understand all state laws, policies and procedures regarding child abuse and neglect. In addition, the parent's attorney must be familiar with the following laws to recognize when they are relevant to a case and should be prepared to research them when they are applicable:

- Titles IV-B and IV-E of the Social Security Act, including the Adoption and Safe Families Act (ASFA), 42 U.S.C. §§ 620-679 and the ASFA Regulations, 45 C.F.R. Parts 1355, 1356, 1357
- Child Abuse Prevention Treatment Act (CAPTA), P.L.108-36
- Indian Child Welfare Act (ICWA) 25 U.S.C. §§ 1901-1963, the ICWA Regulations, 25 C.F.R. Part 23, and the Guidelines for State Courts: Indian Child Custody Proceedings, 44 Fed. Reg. 67, 584 (Nov. 26, 1979)
- State Indian Child Welfare Act laws
- Multi-Ethnic Placement Act (MEPA), as amended by the Inter-Ethnic Adoption Provisions of 1996 (MEPA-IEP) 42 U.S.C. § 622 (b)(9) (1998), 42 U.S.C. § 671(a)(18) (1998), 42 U.S.C. § 1996b (1998).
- Interstate Compact on Placement of Children (ICPC)
- Foster Care Independence Act of 1999 (FCIA), P.L. 106-169
- Individuals with Disabilities Education Act (IDEA), P.L. 91-230
- Family Education Rights Privacy Act (FERPA), 20 U.S.C. § 1232g
- Health Insurance Portability and Accountability Act of 1996 (HIPPA), P. L., 104-192 § 264, 42 U.S.C. § 1320d-2 (in relevant part)
- Public Health Act, 42 U.S.C. Sec. 290dd-2 and 42 C.F.R. Part 2
- Immigration laws relating to child welfare and child custody
- State laws and rules of evidence
- State laws and rules of civil procedure
- State laws and rules of criminal procedure
- State laws concerning privilege and confidentiality, public benefits, education, and disabilities
- State laws and rules of professional responsibility or other relevant ethics standards
- State laws regarding domestic violence
- State domestic relations laws

Commentary
Although the burden of proof is on the child welfare agency, in practice the parent and the parent's attorney generally must demonstrate that the parent can adequately care for the child. The parent's attorney must consider all obstacles to this goal, such as criminal charges against the parent, immigration issues, substance abuse or mental health issues, confidentiality concerns, permanency timelines, and the child's individual service issues. To perform these functions, the parent's

attorney must know enough about all relevant laws to vigorously advocate for the parent's interests. Additionally, the attorney must be able to use procedural, evidentiary and confidentiality laws and rules to protect the parent's rights throughout court proceedings.

3. Understand and protect the parent's rights to information and decision making while the child is in foster care.

Action

The parent's attorney must explain to the parent what decision-making authority remains with the parent and what lies with the child welfare agency while the child is in foster care. The parent's attorney should seek updates and reports from any service provider working with the child/family or help the client obtain information about the child's safety, health, education and well-being when the client desires. Where decision-making rights remain, the parent's attorney should assist the parent in exercising his or her rights to continue to make decisions regarding the child's medical, mental health and educational services. If necessary, the parent's attorney should intervene with the child welfare agency, provider agencies, medical providers and the school to ensure the parent has decision-making opportunities. This may include seeking court orders when the parent has been left out of important decisions about the child's life.

Commentary

Unless and until parental rights are terminated, the parent has parental obligations and rights while a child is in foster care. Advocacy may be necessary to ensure the parent is allowed to remain involved with key aspects of the child's life. Not only should the parent's rights be protected, but continuing to exercise as much parental responsibility as possible is often an effective strategy to speed family reunification. Often, though, a parent does not understand that he or she has the right to help make decisions for, or obtain information about, the child. Therefore, it is the parent's attorney's responsibility to counsel the client and help the parent understand his or her rights and responsibilities and try to assist the parent in carrying them out.

4. Actively represent a parent in the prepetition phase of a case, if permitted within the jurisdiction.

Action

The goal of representing a parent in the prepetition phase of the case is often to deter the agency from deciding to file a petition or to deter the agency from attempting to remove the client's child if a petition is filed. The parent's attorney should counsel the client about the client's rights in the investigation stage as well as the realistic pros and cons of cooperating with the child welfare agency (i.e., the parent's admissions could be used against the client later, but cooperating with services could eliminate a petition filing). The parent's attorney should acknowledge that the parent may be justifiably angry that the agency is involved with the client's family, and help the client develop strategies so the client does not express that anger toward the caseworker in ways that may undermine the client's goals. The attorney should discuss available services and help the client enroll in those in which the client wishes to participate. The attorney should explore conference opportunities with the agency. If it would benefit the client, the attorney should attend any conferences. There are times that an attorney's presence in a conference can shut down discussion, and the attorney should weigh that issue when deciding whether to attend. The attorney should prepare the client for issues that might arise at the conference, such as services and available kinship resources, and discuss with the client the option of bringing a support person to a conference.

Commentary
A few jurisdictions permit parents' attorneys to begin their representation before the child welfare agency files a petition with the court. When the agency becomes involved with the families, it can refer parents to attorneys so that parents will have the benefit of counsel throughout the life of the case. During the prepetition phase, the parent's attorney has the opportunity to work with the parent and help the parent fully understand the issues and the parent's chances of retaining custody of the child. The parent's attorney also has the chance to encourage the agency to make reasonable efforts to work with the family, rather than filing a petition. During this phase, the attorney should work intensively with the parent to explore all appropriate services.

5. **Avoid continuances (or reduce empty adjournments) and work to reduce delays in court proceedings unless there is a strategic benefit for the client.**[3]

Action
The parent's attorney should not request continuances unless there is an emergency or it benefits the client's case. If continuances are necessary, the parent's attorney should request the continuance in writing, as far as possible in advance of the hearing, and should request the shortest delay possible, consistent with the client's interests. The

attorney must notify all counsel of the request. The parent's attorney should object to repeated or prolonged continuance requests by other parties if the continuance would harm the client.

Commentary
Delaying a case often increases the time a family is separated, and can reduce the likelihood of reunification. Appearing in court often motivates parties to comply with orders and cooperate with services. When a judge actively monitors a case, services are often put in place more quickly, visitation may be increased or other requests by the parent may be granted. If a hearing is continued and the case is delayed, the parent may lose momentum in addressing the issues that led to the child's removal or the parent may lose the opportunity to prove compliance with case plan goals. Additionally, the Adoption and Safe Families Act (ASFA) timelines continue to run despite continuances.

6. Cooperate and communicate regularly with other professionals in the case.[4]

Action
The parent's attorney should communicate with attorneys for the other parties, court appointed special advocates (CASAs) or guardians ad litem (GALs). Similarly, the parent's attorney should communicate with the caseworker, foster parents and service providers to learn about the client's progress and their views of the case, as appropriate. The parent's attorney should have open lines of communication with the attorney(s) representing the client in related matters such as any criminal, protection from abuse, private custody or administrative proceedings to ensure that probation orders, protection from abuse orders, private custody orders and administrative determinations do not conflict with the client's goals in the abuse and neglect case.

Commentary
The parent's attorney must have all relevant information to try a case effectively. This requires open and ongoing communication with the other attorneys and service providers working with the client and family. Rules of professional ethics govern contact with represented and unrepresented parties. In some states, for instance, attorneys may not speak with child welfare caseworkers without the permission of agency counsel. The parent's attorney must be aware of local rules on this issue and seek permission to speak with represented parties when that would further the client's interests.

RELATIONSHIP WITH THE CLIENT[5]

7. Advocate for the client's goals and empower the client to direct the representation and make informed decisions based on thorough counsel.[6]

Action

Attorneys representing parents must understand the client's goals and pursue them vigorously. The attorney should explain that the attorney's job is to represent the client's interests and regularly inquire as to the client's goals, including ultimate case goals and interim goals. The attorney should explain all legal aspects of the case and provide comprehensive counsel on the advantages and disadvantages of different options. At the same time, the attorney should be careful not to usurp the client's authority to decide the case goals.

Commentary

Since many clients distrust the child welfare system, the parent's attorney must take care to distinguish him or herself from others in the system so the client can see that the attorney serves the client's interests. The attorney should be mindful that parents often feel disempowered in child welfare proceedings and should take steps to make the client feel comfortable expressing goals and wishes without fear of judgment. The attorney should clearly explain the legal issues as well as expectations of the court and the agency, and potential consequences of the client failing to meet those expectations. The attorney has the responsibility to provide expertise, and to make strategic decisions about the best ways to achieve the parent's goals, but the client is in charge of deciding the case goals and the attorney must act accordingly.

8. Act in accordance with the duty of loyalty owed to the client.

Action

Attorneys representing parents should show respect and professionalism towards their clients. Parents' attorneys should support their clients and be sensitive to the client's individual needs. Attorneys should remember that they may be the client's only advocate in the system and should act accordingly.

Commentary

Often attorneys practicing in abuse and neglect court are a close-knit group who work and sometimes socialize together. Maintaining good working relationships with other players in the child welfare system is an important part of being an effective advocate. The attorney, however, should be vigilant against allowing the attorney's own interests in relationships with others in the system to interfere with the attorney's primary responsibility to the client. The attorneys should not give the impression to the client that relationships with other attorneys are more important than the representation the attorney is providing the client. The client must feel that the attorney believes in him or her and is actively advocating on the client's behalf.

9. Adhere to all laws and ethical obligations concerning confidentiality.[7]

Action
Attorneys representing parents must understand confidentiality laws, as well as ethical obligations, and adhere to both with respect to information obtained from or about the client. The attorney must fully explain to the client the advantages and disadvantages of choosing to exercise, partially waive, or waive a privilege or right to confidentiality. Consistent with the client's interests and goals, the attorney must seek to protect from disclosure confidential information concerning the client.

Commentary
Confidential information contained in a parent's substance abuse treatment records, domestic violence treatment records, mental health records and medical records is often at issue in abuse and neglect cases. Improper disclosure of confidential information early in the proceeding may have a negative impact on the manner in which the client is perceived by the other parties and the court. For this reason, it is crucial for the attorney to advise the client promptly as to the advantages and disadvantages of releasing confidential information, and for the attorney to take whatever steps necessary to protect the client's privileges or rights to confidentiality.

10. Provide the client with contact information in writing and establish a message system that allows regular attorney-client contact.[8]

Action
The parent's attorney should ensure the parent understands how to contact the attorney and that the attorney wants to hear from the client on an ongoing basis. The attorney should explain that even when the attorney is unavailable, the parent should leave a message. The attorney must respond to client messages in a reasonable time period. The attorney and client should establish a reliable communication system that meets the client's needs. For example, it may involve telephone

contact, email or communication through a third party when the client agrees to it. Interpreters should be used when the attorney and client are not fluent in the same language.

Commentary

Gaining the client's trust and establishing ongoing communication are two essential aspects of representing the parent. The parent may feel angry and believe that all of the attorneys in the system work with the child welfare agency and against that parent. It is important that the parent's attorney, from the beginning of the case, is clear with the parent that the attorney works for the parent, is available for consultation, and wants to communicate regularly. This will help the attorney support the client, gather information for the case and learn of any difficulties the parent is experiencing that the attorney might help address. The attorney should explain to the client the benefits of bringing issues to the attorney's attention rather than letting problems persist. The attorney should also explain that the attorney is available to intervene when the client's relationship with the agency or provider is not working effectively. The attorney should be aware of the client's circumstances, such as whether the client has access to a telephone, and tailor the communication system to the individual client.

11. **Meet and communicate regularly with the client well before court proceedings. Counsel the client about all legal matters related to the case, including specific allegations against the client, the service plan, the client's rights in the pending proceeding, any orders entered against the client and the potential consequences of failing to obey court orders or cooperate with service plans.**[9]

Action

The parent's attorney should spend time with the client to prepare the case and address questions and concerns. The attorney should clearly explain the allegations made against the parent, what is likely to happen before, during and after each hearing, and what steps the parent can take to increase the likelihood of reuniting with the child. The attorney should explain any settlement options and determine whether the client wants the attorney to pursue such options. The attorney should explain courtroom procedures. The attorney should write to the client to ensure the client understands what happened in court and what is expected of the client.

The attorney should ensure a formal interpreter is involved when the attorney and client are not fluent in the same language. The attorney should advocate for the use of an interpreter when other professionals in the case who are not fluent in the same language as the client are interviewing the client as well.

The attorney should be available for in-person meetings or telephone calls to answer the client's questions and address the client's concerns. The attorney and client should work together to identify and review short and long-term goals, particularly as circumstances change during the case.

The parent's attorney should help the client access information about the child's developmental and other needs by speaking to service providers and reviewing the child's records. The parent needs to understand these issues to make appropriate decisions for the child's care.

The parent's attorney and the client should identify barriers to the client engaging in services, such as employment, transportation, and financial issues. The attorney should work with the client, caseworker and service provider to resolve the barriers.

The attorney should be aware of any special issues the parents may have related to participating in the proposed case plan, such as an inability to read or language differences, and advocate with the child welfare agency and court for appropriate accommodations.

Commentary
The parent's attorney's job extends beyond the courtroom. The attorney should be a counselor as well as litigator. The attorney should be available to talk with the client to prepare for hearings, and to provide advice and information about ongoing concerns. Open lines of communication between attorneys and clients help ensure clients get answers to questions and attorneys get the information and documents they need.

12. Work with the client to develop a case timeline and tickler system.

Action
At the beginning of a case, the parent's attorney and client should develop timelines that reflect projected deadlines and important dates and a tickler/calendar system to remember the dates. The timeline should specify what actions the attorney and parent will need to take and dates by which they will be completed. The attorney and the client should know when important dates will occur and should be focused on accomplishing the objectives in the case plan in a timely way. The attorney should provide the client with a timeline/calendar, outlining

known and prospective court dates, service appointments, deadlines and critical points of attorney-client contact. The attorney should record federal and state law deadlines in the system (e.g., the 15 of 22 month point that would necessitate a termination of parental rights (TPR), if exceptions do not apply).

Commentary

Having a consistent calendaring system can help an attorney manage a busy caseload. Clients should receive a hard copy calendar to keep track of appointments and important dates. This helps parents stay focused on accomplishing the service plan goals and meeting court-imposed deadlines.

13. **Provide the client with copies of all petitions, court orders, service plans, and other relevant case documents, including reports regarding the child except when expressly prohibited by law, rule or court order.**[10]

Action

The parent's attorney should provide all written documents to the client or ensure that they are provided in a timely manner and ensure the client understands them. If the client has difficulty reading, the attorney should read the documents to the client. In all cases, the attorney should be available to discuss and explain the documents to the client.

Commentary

The parent's attorney should ensure the client is informed about what is happening in the case. Part of doing so is providing the client with written documents and reports relevant to the case. If the client has this information, the client will be better able to assist the attorney with the case and fulfill his or her parental obligations. The attorney must be aware of any allegations of domestic violence in the case and not share confidential information about an alleged or potential victim's location.

14. **Be alert to and avoid potential conflicts of interest or the appearance of a conflict of interest that would interfere with the competent representation of the client.**[11]

Action

The parent's attorney must not represent both parents if their interests differ. The attorney should generally avoid representing both parents when there is even a potential for conflicts of interests. In situations involving allegations of domestic violence the attorney should never represent both parents.

Commentary

In most cases, attorneys should avoid representing both parents in an abuse or neglect case. In the rare case in which an attorney, after careful consideration of potential conflicts, may represent both parents, it should only be with their informed consent. Even in cases in which there is no apparent conflict at the beginning of the case, conflicts may arise as the case proceeds. If this occurs, the attorney might be required to withdraw from representing one or both parents. This could be difficult for the clients and delay the case. Other examples of potential conflicts of interest that the attorney should avoid include representing multiple fathers in the same case or representing parties in a separate case who have interests in the current case.

In analyzing whether a conflict of interest exists, the attorney must consider "whether pursuing one client's objectives will prevent the lawyer from pursuing another client's objectives, and whether confidentiality may be compromised."[12]

15. **Act in a culturally competent manner and with regard to the socioeconomic position of the parent throughout all aspects of representation.**

Action

The parent's attorney should learn about and understand the client's background, determine how that has an impact on the client's case, and always show the parent respect. The attorney must understand how cultural and socioeconomic differences impact interaction with clients, and must interpret the client's words and actions accordingly.

Commentary

The child welfare system is comprised of a diverse group of people, including the clients and professionals involved. Each person comes to this system with his or her own set of values and expectations, but it is essential that each person try to learn about and understand the backgrounds of others. An individual's race, ethnicity, gender, sexual orientation and socioeconomic position all have an impact on how the person acts and reacts in particular situations. The parent's attorney must be vigilant against imposing the attorney's values onto the clients, and should, instead, work with the parents within the context of their culture and socioeconomic position. While the court and child welfare agency have expectations of parents in their treatment of children, the parent's advocate must strive to explain these expectations to the clients in a sensitive way. The parent's attorney should also try to explain how the client's background might affect the client's ability to comply with court orders and agency requests.

16. **Take diligent steps to locate and communicate with a missing parent and decide representation strategies based on that communication.**[13]

Action
Upon accepting an appointment, the parent's attorney should communicate to the client the importance of staying in contact with the attorney. While the attorney must communicate regularly with the client, and be informed of the client's wishes before a hearing, the client also must keep in contact with the attorney. At the beginning of the representation, the attorney should tell the client how to contact the attorney, and discuss the importance of the client keeping the attorney informed of changes in address, phone numbers, and the client's current whereabouts.

The parent's attorney should attempt to locate and communicate with missing parents to formulate what positions the attorney should take at hearings, and to understand what information the client wishes the attorney to share with the child welfare agency and the court. If, after diligent steps, the attorney is unable to communicate with the client, the attorney should assess whether the client's interests are better served by advocating for the client's last clearly articulated position, or declining to participate in further court proceedings, and should act accordingly. After a prolonged period without contact with the client, the attorney should consider withdrawing from representation.

Commentary
Diligent Steps to Locate: To represent a client adequately, the attorney must know what the client wishes. It is, therefore, important for parents' attorneys to take diligent steps to locate missing clients. Diligent steps can include speaking with the client's family, the caseworker, the foster care provider and other service providers. It should include contacting the State Department of Corrections, Social Security Administration, and Child Support Office, and sending letters by regular and certified mail to the client's last known address. The attorney should also visit the client's last known address and asking anyone who lives there for information about the client's whereabouts. Additionally, the attorney should leave business cards with contact information with anyone who might have contact with the client as long as this does not compromise confidentiality.

Unsuccessful Efforts to Locate: If the attorney is unable to find and communicate with the client after initial consultation, the attorney should assess what action would best serve the client's interests. This decision must be made on a case-by-case basis. In some cases, the attorney may decide to take a position consistent with the client's last clearly articulated position. In other cases the client's interests may be better served by the attorney declining to participate in the court proceedings in the absence of the client because that may better protect the client's right to vacate orders made in the client's absence.

17. Be aware of the unique issues an incarcerated parent faces and provide competent representation to the incarcerated client.

Action
Adoption and Safe Families Act (ASFA) Issues: The parent's attorney must be particularly diligent when representing an incarcerated parent. The attorney must be aware of the reasons for the incarceration. If the parent is incarcerated as a result of an act against the child or another child in the family, the child welfare agency may request an order from the court that reasonable efforts toward reunification are not necessary and attempt to fast-track the case toward other permanency goals. If this is the case, the attorney must be prepared to argue against such a motion, if the client opposes it. Even if no motion is made to waive the reasonable efforts requirement, in some jurisdictions the agency may not have the same obligations to assist parents who are incarcerated. Attorneys should counsel the client as to any effects incarceration has on the agency's obligations and know the jurisdiction's statutory and case law concerning incarceration as a basis for TPR. The attorney should help the client identify potential kinship placements, relatives who can provide care for the child while the parent is incarcerated. States vary in whether and how they weigh factors such as the reason for incarceration, length of incarceration and the child's age at the time of incarceration when considering TPR. Attorneys must understand the implications of ASFA for an incarcerated parent who has difficulty visiting and planning for the child.

Services: Obtaining services such as substance abuse treatment, parenting skills, or job training while in jail or prison is often difficult. The parent's attorney may need to advocate for reasonable efforts to be made for the client, and assist the parent and the agency caseworker in accessing services. The attorney must assist the client with these services. Without services, it is unlikely the parent will be reunified with the child upon discharge from prison.

If the attorney practices in a jurisdiction that has a specialized unit for parents and children, and especially when the client is incarcerated for an offense that is unrelated to the child, the attorney should advocate for such a placement. The attorney must learn about available resources, contact the placements and attempt to get the support of the agency and child's attorney.

Communication: The parent's attorney should counsel the client on the importance of maintaining regular contact with the child while incarcerated. The attorney should assist in developing a plan for communication and visitation by obtaining necessary court orders and working with the caseworker as well as the correctional facility's social worker.

If the client cannot meet the attorney before court hearings, the attorney must find alternative ways to communicate. This may include visiting the client in prison or engaging in more extensive phone or mail contact than with other clients. The attorney should be aware of the challenges to having a confidential conversation with the client, and attempt to resolve that issue.

The parent's attorney should also communicate with the parent's criminal defense attorney. There may be issues related to self-incrimination as well as concerns about delaying the abuse and neglect case to strengthen the criminal case or vice versa.

Appearance in Court: The client's appearance in court frequently raises issues that require the attorney's attention in advance. The attorney should find out from the client if the client wants to be present in court. In some prisons, inmates lose privileges if they are away from the prison, and the client may prefer to stay at the prison. If the client wants to be present in court, the attorney should work with the court to obtain a writ of habeas corpus/bring-down order/order to produce or other documentation necessary for the client to be transported from the prison. The attorney should explain to any client hesitant to appear, that the case will proceed without the parent's presence and raise any potential consequences of that choice. If the client does not want to be present, or if having the client present is not possible, the attorney should be educated about what means are available to have the client participate, such as by telephone or video conference. The attorney should make the necessary arrangements for the client. Note that it may be particularly difficult to get a parent transported from an out-of-state prison or a federal prison.

18. Be aware of the client's mental health status and be prepared to assess whether the parent can assist with the case.

Action
Attorneys representing parents must be able to determine whether a client's mental status (including mental illness and mental

retardation) interferes with the client's ability to make decisions about the case. The attorney should be familiar with any mental health diagnosis and treatment that a client has had in the past or is presently undergoing (including any medications for such conditions). The attorney should get consent from the client to review mental health records and to speak with former and current mental health providers. The attorney should explain to the client that the information is necessary to understand the client's capacity to work with the attorney. If the client's situation seems severe, the attorney should also explain that the attorney may seek the assistance of a clinical social worker or some other mental health expert to evaluate the client's ability to assist the attorney because if the client does not have that capacity, the attorney may have to ask that a guardian ad litem be appointed to the client. Since this action may have an adverse effect on the client's legal claims, the attorney should ask for a GAL only when absolutely necessary.

Commentary

Many parents charged with abuse and neglect have serious or long-standing mental health challenges. However, not all of those conditions or diagnoses preclude the client from participating in the defense. Whether the client can assist counsel is a different issue from whether the client is able to parent the children, though the condition may be related to ability to parent. While the attorney is not expected to be a mental health expert, the attorney should be familiar with mental health conditions and should review such records carefully. The fact that a client suffers a disability does not diminish the lawyer's obligation to treat the client with attention and respect. If the client seems unable to assist the attorney in case preparation, the attorney should seek an assessment of the client's capacity from a mental health expert. If the expert and attorney conclude that the client is not capable of assisting in the case, the attorney should inform the client that the attorney will seek appointment of a guardian ad litem from the court. The attorney should be careful to explain that the attorney will still represent the client in the child protective case. The attorney must explain to the client that appointment of a GAL will limit the client's decision-making power. The GAL will stand in the client's shoes for that purpose.

Investigation[14]

19. **Conduct a thorough and independent investigation at every stage of the proceeding.**

Action

The parent's attorney must take all necessary steps to prepare each case. A thorough investigation is an essential element of preparation. The parent's attorney can not rely solely on what the agency case-worker reports about the parent. Rather, the attorney should contact service providers who work with the client, relatives who can discuss the parent's care of the child, the child's teacher or other people who can clarify information relevant to the case. If necessary, the attorney should petition the court for funds to hire an investigator.

Commentary

In some jurisdictions, parents' attorneys work with social workers or investigators who can meet with clients and assist in investigating the underlying issues that arise as cases proceed. The drafting committee recommends such a model of representation. However, if the attorney is not working with such a team, the attorney is still responsible for gaining all pertinent case information.

20. Interview the client well before each hearing, in time to use client information for the case investigation.[15]

Action

The parent's attorney should meet with the parent regularly throughout the case. The meetings should occur well before the hearing, not at the courthouse just minutes before the case is called before the judge. The attorney should ask the client questions to obtain information to prepare the case, and strive to create a comfortable environment so the client can ask the attorney questions. The attorney should use these meetings to prepare for court as well as to counsel the client concerning issues that arise during the course of the case. Information obtained from the client should be used to propel the investigation.

Commentary

Often, the client is the best source of information for the attorney, and the attorney should set aside time to obtain that information. Since the interview may involve disclosure of sensitive or painful information, the attorney should explain attorney-client confidentiality to the client. The attorney may need to work hard to gain the client's trust, but if a trusting relationship can be developed, the attorney will have an easier time representing the client. The investigation will be more effective if guided by the client, as the client generally knows firsthand what occurred in the case.

Informal Discovery[16]

21. Review the child welfare agency case file.

Action
The parent's attorney should ask for and review the agency case file as early during the course of representation as possible. The file contains useful documents that the attorney may not yet have, and will instruct the attorney on the agency's case theory. If the agency case file is inaccurate, the attorney should seek to correct it. The attorney must read the case file periodically because information is continually being added by the agency.

Commentary
While an independent investigation is essential, it is also important that the parent's attorney understands what information the agency is relying on to further its case. The case file should contain a history about the family that the client may not have shared, and important reports and information about both the child and parent that will be necessary for the parent's attorney to understand for hearings as well as settlement conferences. Unless the attorney also has the information the agency has, the parent's attorney will walk into court at a disadvantage.

22. Obtain all necessary documents, including copies of all pleadings and relevant notices filed by other parties, and information from the caseworker and providers.

Action
As part of the discovery phase, the parent's attorney should gather all relevant documentation regarding the case that might shed light on the allegations, the service plan and the client's strengths as a parent. The attorney should not limit the scope as information about past or present criminal, protection from abuse, private custody or administrative proceedings involving the client can have an impact on the abuse and neglect case. The attorney should also review the following kinds of documents:

- social service records
- court records
- medical records
- school records
- evaluations of all types

The attorney should be sure to obtain reports and records from service providers.

Discovery is not limited to information regarding the client, but may include records of others such as the other parent, stepparent, child, relative and non-relative caregivers.

Commentary
In preparing the client's case, the attorney must try to learn as much about the parent and the family as possible. Various records may contradict or supplement the agency's account of events. Gathering documentation to verify the client's reports about what occurred before the child came into care and progress the parent is making during the case is necessary to provide concrete evidence for the court. Documentation may also alert the attorney to issues the client is having that the client did not share with counsel. The attorney may be able to intercede and assist the client with service providers, agency caseworkers and others.

Formal Discovery[17]

> **23. When needed, use formal discovery methods to obtain information.**

Action
The parent's attorney should know what information is needed to prepare for the case and understand the best methods of obtaining that information. The attorney should become familiar with the pretrial requests and actions used in the jurisdiction and use whatever tools are available to obtain necessary information. The parent's attorney should consider the following types of formal discovery: depositions, interrogatories (including expert interrogatories), requests for production of documents, requests for admissions, and motions for mental or physical examination of a party. The attorney should file timely motions for discovery and renew these motions as needed to obtain the most recent records.

The attorney should, consistent with the client's interests and goals, and where appropriate, take all necessary steps to preserve and protect the client's rights by opposing discovery requests of other parties.

Court Preparation[18]

> **24. Develop a case theory and strategy to follow at hearings and negotiations.**

Action
Once the parent's attorney has completed the initial investigation and discovery, including interviews with the client, the attorney

should develop a strategy for representation. The strategy may change throughout the case, as the client makes or does not make progress, but the initial theory is important to assist the attorney in staying focused on the client's wishes and on what is achievable. The theory of the case should inform the attorney's preparation for hearings and arguments to the court throughout the case. It should also help the attorney decide what evidence to develop for hearings and the steps to take to move the case toward the client's ultimate goals (e.g., requesting increased visitation when a parent becomes engaged in services).

25. Timely file all pleadings, motions, and briefs. Research applicable legal issues and advance legal arguments when appropriate.

Action
The attorney must file petitions, motions, discovery requests, and responses and answers to pleadings filed by other parties that are appropriate for the case. These pleadings must be thorough, accurate and timely.

When a case presents a complicated or new legal issue, the parent's attorney should conduct the appropriate research before appearing in court. The attorney must have a solid understanding of the relevant law, and be able to present it to the judge in a compelling and convincing way. The attorney should be prepared to distinguish case law that appears to be unfavorable. If the judge asks for memoranda of law, the attorney will already have done the research and will be able to use it to argue the case well. If it would advance the client's case, the parent's attorney should present an unsolicited memorandum of law to the court.

Commentary
Actively filing motions, pleadings and briefs benefits the client. This practice puts important issues before the court and builds credibility for the attorney. In addition to filing responsive papers and discovery requests, the attorney should proactively seek court orders that benefit the client, e.g., filing a motion to enforce court orders to ensure the child welfare agency is meeting its reasonable efforts obligations. When an issue arises, it is often appropriate to attempt to resolve it informally with other parties. When out-of-court advocacy is not successful, the attorney should not wait to bring the issue to the court's attention if that would serve the client's goals.

Arguments in child welfare cases are often fact-based. Nonetheless, attorneys should ground their arguments in statutory, regulatory and common law. These sources of law exist in each jurisdiction, as well as in federal law. Additionally, law from other jurisdictions can be used to sway a court in the client's favor. An attorney who has a firm grasp of the law, and who is willing to do legal research on an individual case, may have more credibility before the court. At times, competent representation requires advancing legal arguments that are not yet accepted in the jurisdiction. Attorneys should be mindful to preserve issues for appellate review by making a record even if the argument is unlikely to prevail at the trial level

> **26. Engage in case planning and advocate for appropriate social services using a multidisciplinary approach to representation when available.**

Action

The parent's attorney must advocate for the client both in and out of court. The parent's attorney should know about the social, mental health, substance abuse treatment and other services that are available to parents and families in the jurisdiction in which the attorney practices so the attorney can advocate effectively for the client to receive these services. The attorney should ask the client if the client wishes to engage in services. If so, the attorney must determine whether the client has access to the necessary services to overcome the issues that led to the case.

The attorney should actively engage in case planning, including attending major case meetings, to ensure the client asks for and receives the needed services. The attorney should also ensure the client does not agree to undesired services that are beyond the scope of the case. A major case meeting is one in which the attorney or client believes the attorney will be needed to provide advice or one in which a major decision on legal steps, such as a change in the child's permanency goal, will be made. The attorney should be available to accompany the client to important meetings with service providers as needed.

The services in which the client is involved must be tailored to the client's needs, and not merely hurdles over which the client must jump (e.g., if the client is taking parenting classes, the classes must be relevant to the underlying issue in the case).

Whenever possible, the parent's attorney should engage or involve a social worker as part of the parent's "team" to help determine an appropriate case plan, evaluate social services suggested for the client, and act as a liaison and advocate for the client with the service providers.

When necessary, the parent's attorney should seek court orders to force the child welfare agency to provide services or visitation to the client. The attorney may need to ask the court to enforce previously entered orders that the agency did not comply with in a reasonable period. The attorney should consider whether the child's representative (lawyer, GAL or CASA) might be an ally on service and visitation issues. If so, the attorney should solicit the child's representative's assistance and work together in making requests to the agency and the court.

Commentary

For a parent to succeed in a child welfare case the parent must receive and cooperate with social services. It is therefore necessary that the parent's attorney does whatever possible to obtain appropriate services for the client, and then counsel the client about participating in such services. Examples of services common to child welfare cases include:

- Evaluations
- Family preservation or reunification services
- Medical and mental health care
- Drug and alcohol treatment
- Domestic violence prevention, intervention or treatment
- Parenting education
- Education and job training
- Housing
- Child care
- Funds for public transportation so the client can attend services

27. Aggressively advocate for regular visitation in a family-friendly setting.

Action

The parent's attorney should advocate for an effective visiting plan and counsel the parent on the importance of regular contact with the child. Preservation of parent-child bonds through regular visitation is essential to any reunification effort. Courts and child welfare agencies may need to be pushed to develop visiting plans that best fit the needs of the individual family. Factors to consider in visiting plans include:

- Frequency
- Length
- Location
- Supervision

- Types of activities
- Visit coaching—having someone at the visit who could model effective parenting skills

Commentary

Consistent, high quality visitation is one of the best predictors of successful reunification between a parent and child. Often visits are arranged in settings that are uncomfortable and inhibiting for families. It is important that the parent's attorney seek a visitation order that will allow the best possible visitation. Effort should be made to have visits be unsupervised or at the lowest possible level of supervision. Families are often more comfortable when relatives, family friends, clergy or other community members are recruited to supervise visits rather than caseworkers. Attorneys should advocate for visits to occur in the most family-friendly locations possible, such as in the family's home, parks, libraries, restaurants, places of worship or other community venues.

28. With the client's permission, and when appropriate, engage in settlement negotiations and mediation to resolve the case.

Action

The parent's attorney should, when appropriate, participate in settlement negotiations to promptly resolve the case, keeping in mind the effect of continuances and delays on the client's goals. Parents' attorneys should be trained in mediation and negotiation skills and be comfortable resolving cases outside a courtroom setting when consistent with the client's position. When authorized to do so by the client, the parent's attorney should share information about services in which the parent is engaged and provide copies of favorable reports from service providers. This information may impact settlement discussions. The attorney must communicate all settlement offers to the client and discuss their advantages and disadvantages. It is the client's decision whether to settle. The attorney must be willing to try the case and not compromise solely to avoid the hearing. The attorney should use mediation resources when available.

Commentary

Negotiation and mediation often result in a detailed agreement among parties about actions the participants must take. Generally, when agreements have been thoroughly discussed and negotiated, all parties, including the parents, feel as if they had a say in the decision and are, therefore, more willing to adhere to a plan. Mediation can resolve a specific conflict in a case, even if it does not result in an agreement about the entire case. Negotiated settlements generally happen more quickly than full hearings and therefore move a case along swiftly. The attorney should discuss all aspects of proposed settlements with the parent, including all legal effects of admissions or agreements. The attorney should advise the client about the chances of prevailing if the matter proceeds to trial and any potential negative impact associated with contesting the allegations. The final decision regarding settlement must be the client's.

A written, enforceable agreement should result from any settlement, so all parties are clear about their rights and obligations. The parent's attorney should ensure agreements accurately reflect the understandings of the parties. The parent's attorney should schedule a hearing if promises made to the parent are not kept.

29. Thoroughly prepare the client to testify at the hearing.

Action
When having the client testify will benefit the case or when the client wishes to testify, the parent's attorney should thoroughly prepare the client. The attorney should discuss and practice the questions that the attorney will ask the client, as well as the types of questions the client should expect opposing counsel to ask. The parent's attorney should help the parent think through the best way to present information, familiarize the parent with the court setting, and offer guidance on logistical issues such as how to get to court on time and appropriate court attire.

Commentary
Testifying in court can be intimidating. For a parent whose family is the focus of the proceeding, the court experience is even scarier. The parent's attorney should be attuned to the client's comfort level about the hearing, and ability to testify in the case. The attorney should spend time explaining the process and the testimony itself to the client. The attorney should provide the client with a written list of questions that the attorney will ask, if this will help the client.

30. Identify, locate and prepare all witnesses.

Action
The parent's attorney, in consultation with the parent, should develop a witness list well before a hearing. The attorney should not assume the agency will call a witness, even if the witness is named on the agency's

witness list. The attorney should, when possible, contact the potential witnesses to determine if they can provide helpful testimony.

When appropriate, witnesses should be informed that a subpoena is on its way. The attorney should also ensure the subpoena is served. The attorney should subpoena potential agency witnesses (e.g., a previous caseworker) who have favorable information about the client.

The attorney should set aside time to fully prepare all witnesses in person before the hearing. The attorney should remind the witnesses about the court date.

Commentary

Preparation is the key to successfully resolving a case, either in negotiation or trial. The attorney should plan as early as possible for the case and make arrangements accordingly. Witnesses may have direct knowledge of the allegations against the parent. They may be service providers working with the parent, or individuals from the community who could testify generally about the family's strengths.

When appropriate, the parent's attorney should consider working with other parties who share the parent's position (such as the child's representative) when creating a witness list, issuing subpoenas, and preparing witnesses. Doctors, nurses, teachers, therapists, and other potential witnesses have busy schedules and need advance warning about the date and time of the hearing.

Witnesses are often nervous about testifying in court. Attorneys should prepare them thoroughly so they feel comfortable with the process. Preparation will generally include rehearsing the specific questions and answers expected on direct and anticipating the questions and answers that might arise on cross-examination. Attorneys should provide written questions for those witnesses who need them.

31. Identify, secure, prepare and qualify expert witness when needed. When permissible, interview opposing counsel's experts.

Action

Often a case requires multiple experts in different roles, such as experts in medicine, mental health treatment, drug and alcohol treatment, or social work. Experts may be needed for ongoing case consultation in addition to providing testimony at trial. The attorney should consider whether the opposing party is calling expert witnesses and determine whether the parent needs to call any experts.

When expert testimony is required, the attorney should identify the qualified experts and seek necessary funds to retain them in a timely manner. The attorney should subpoena the witnesses, giving them as much advanced notice of the court date as possible. As is true for all witnesses, the attorney should spend as much time as possible preparing the expert witnesses for the hearing. The attorney should be competent in qualifying expert witnesses.

When opposing counsel plans to call expert witnesses, the parent's attorney should file expert interrogatories, depose the witnesses or interview the witnesses in advance, depending on the jurisdiction's rules on attorney work product. The attorney should do whatever is necessary to learn what the opposing expert witnesses will say about the client during the hearing.

Commentary
By contacting opposing counsel's expert witnesses in advance, the parent's attorney will know what evidence will be presented against the client and whether the expert has any favorable information that might be elicited on cross-examination. The attorney will be able to discuss the issues with the client, prepare a defense and call experts on behalf of the client, if appropriate. Conversely, if the attorney does not talk to the opposing expert in advance, the attorney could be surprised by the evidence and unable to represent the client competently.

Hearings

32. Attend and prepare for all hearings, including pretrial conferences.

Action
The parent's attorney must prepare for, and attend all hearings and participate in all telephone and other conferences with the court.

Commentary
For the parent to have a fair chance during the hearing, the attorney must be prepared and present in court. Participating in pretrial proceedings may improve case resolution for the parent. Counsel's failure to participate in the proceedings in which all other parties are represented may disadvantage the parent. Therefore, the parent's attorney should be actively involved in this stage. Other than in extraordinary circumstances, attorneys must appear for all court appearances on time. In many jurisdictions, if an attorney arrives to court late, or not at all, the case will receive a long continuance. This does not serve the client and does not instill confidence in the attorney. If an attorney has a conflict with another courtroom appearance, the attorney should

notify the court and other parties and request a short continuance. The parent's attorney should not have another attorney stand in to represent the client in a substantive hearing, especially if the other attorney is unfamiliar with the client or case.

33. Prepare and make all appropriate motions and evidentiary objections.

Action

The parent's attorney should make appropriate motions and evidentiary objections to advance the client's position during the hearing. If necessary, the attorney should file briefs in support of the client's position on motions and evidentiary issues. The parent's attorney should always be aware of preserving legal issues for appeal.

Commentary

It is essential that parents' attorneys understand the applicable rules of evidence and all court rules and procedures. The attorney must be willing and able to make appropriate motions, objections, and arguments (e.g., objecting to the qualification of expert witnesses or raising the issue of the child welfare agency's lack of reasonable efforts).

34. Present and cross-examine witnesses, prepare and present exhibits.

Action

The parent's attorney must be able to present witnesses effectively to advance the client's position. Witnesses must be prepared in advance and the attorney should know what evidence will be presented through the witnesses. The attorney must also be skilled at cross-examining opposing parties' witnesses. The attorney must know how to offer documents, photos and physical objects into evidence.

   At each hearing the attorney should keep the case theory in mind, advocate for the child to return home and for appropriate services, if that is the client's position, and request that the court state its expectations of all parties.

Commentary

Becoming a strong courtroom attorney takes practice and attention to detail. The attorney must be sure to learn the rules about presenting witnesses, impeaching testimony, and entering evidence. The attorney should seek out training in trial skills and observe more experienced trial attorneys to learn from them. Even if the parent's attorney is more seasoned, effective direct and cross-examination require careful preparation. The attorney must know the relevant records well enough to be able to impeach adverse witnesses and bring out in both direct and cross examinations any information that would support the parent's position. Seasoned attorneys may wish to consult with other experienced attorneys about complex cases. Presenting and cross-examining witnesses are skills with which the parent's attorney must be comfortable.

35. In jurisdictions in which a jury trial is possible, actively participate in jury selection and drafting jury instructions.

Commentary
Several jurisdictions around the country afford parties in child welfare cases the right to a jury trial at the adjudicatory or termination of parental rights stages. Parents' attorneys in those jurisdictions should be skilled at choosing an appropriate jury, drafting jury instructions that are favorable to the client's position, and trying the case before jurors who may not be familiar with child abuse and neglect issues.

36. Request closed proceedings (or a cleared courtroom) in appropriate cases.

Action
The parent's attorney should be aware of who is in the courtroom during a hearing, and should request the courtroom be cleared of individuals not related to the case when appropriate. The attorney should be attuned to the client's comfort level with people outside of the case hearing about the client's family. The attorney should also be aware of whether the case is one in which there is media attention. Confidential information should not be discussed in front of the media or others without the express permission of the client.

Commentary
In many courts, even if they have a "closed court" policy, attorneys, caseworkers, and witnesses on other cases listed that day may be waiting in the courtroom. These individuals may make the client uncomfortable, and the parent's attorney should request that the judge remove them from the courtroom. Even in an "open court" jurisdiction, there may be cases, or portions of cases, that outsiders should not be permitted to hear. The parent's attorney must be attuned to this issue, and make appropriate requests of the judge.

37. Request the opportunity to make opening and closing arguments.

Action

When permitted by the judge, the parent's attorney should make opening and closing arguments to best present the parent's attorney's theory of the case.

Commentary

In many child abuse and neglect proceedings, attorneys waive the opportunity to make opening and closing arguments. However, these arguments can help shape the way the judge views the case, and therefore can help the client. Argument may be especially critical, for example, in complicated cases when information from expert witnesses should be highlighted for the judge, in hearings that take place over a number of days, or when there are several children and the agency is requesting different services or permanency goals for each of them. Making opening and closing argument is particularly important if the case is being heard by a jury.

38. Prepare proposed findings of fact, conclusions of law and orders when they will be used in the court's decision or may otherwise benefit the client.

Action

Proposed findings of fact, conclusions of law, and orders should be prepared before a hearing. When the judge is prepared to enter a ruling, the judge can use the proposed findings or amend them as needed.

Commentary

By preparing proposed findings of fact and conclusions of law, the parent's attorney frames the case and ruling for the judge. This may result in orders that are more favorable to the parent, preserve appellate issues, and help the attorney clarify desired outcomes before a hearing begins. The attorney should offer to provide the judge with proposed findings and orders in electronic format. If an opposing party prepared the order, the parent's attorney should review it for accuracy before the order is submitted for the judge's signature.

Post Hearings/Appeals

39. Review court orders to ensure accuracy and clarity and review with client.

Action

After the hearing, the parent's attorney should review the written order to ensure it reflects the court's verbal order. If the order is incorrect, the attorney should take whatever steps are necessary to correct it. Once the order is final, the parent's attorney should provide the client with a copy of the order and should review the order with the client to ensure the client understands it. If the client is unhappy with the order, the attorney should counsel the client about any options to appeal or request rehearing on the order, but should explain that the order is in effect unless a stay or other relief is secured. The attorney should counsel the client on the potential consequences of failing to comply with a court order.

Commentary

The parent may be angry about being involved in the child welfare system, and a court order that is not in the parent's favor could add stress and frustration. It is essential that the parent's attorney take time, either immediately after the hearing or at a meeting soon after the court date, to discuss the hearing and the outcome with the client. The attorney should counsel the client about all options, including appeal (see 41). Regardless of whether an appeal is appropriate, the attorney should counsel the parent about potential consequences of not complying with the order.

40. Take reasonable steps to ensure the client complies with court orders and to determine whether the case needs to be brought back to court.

Action

The parent's attorney should answer the parent's questions about obligations under the order and periodically check with the client to determine the client's progress in implementing the order. If the client is attempting to comply with the order but other parties, such as the child welfare agency, are not meeting their responsibilities, the parent's attorney should approach the other party and seek assistance on behalf of the client. If necessary, the attorney should bring the case back to court to review the order and the other party's noncompliance or take other steps to ensure that appropriate social services are available to the client.

Commentary

The parent's attorney should play an active role in assisting the client in complying with court orders and obtaining visitation and any other social services. The attorney should speak with the client regularly about progress and any difficulties the client is encountering while trying to comply with the court order or service plan. When the child welfare agency does not offer appropriate services, the attorney should consider making referrals to social service providers and, when possible, retaining a social worker to assist the client. The drafting committee of these standards recommends such an interdisciplinary model of practice.

41. Consider and discuss the possibility of appeal with the client.[19]

Action

The parent's attorney should consider and discuss with the client the possibility of appeal when a court's ruling is contrary to the client's position or interests. The attorney should counsel the client on the likelihood of success on appeal and potential consequences of an appeal. In most jurisdictions, the decision whether to appeal is the client's as long as a non-frivolous legal basis for appeal exists. Depending on rules in the attorney's jurisdiction, the attorney should also consider filing an extraordinary writ or motions for other post-hearing relief.

Commentary

When discussing the possibility of an appeal, the attorney should explain both the positive and negative effects of an appeal, including how the appeal could affect the parent's goals. For instance, an appeal could delay the case for a long time. This could negatively impact both the parent and the child.

42. If the client decides to appeal, timely and thoroughly file the necessary post-hearing motions and paperwork related to the appeal and closely follow the jurisdiction's Rules of Appellate Procedure.

Action

The parent's attorney should carefully review his or her obligations under the state's Rules of Appellate Procedure. The attorney should timely file all paperwork, including a notice of appeal and requests for stays of the trial court order, transcript, and case file. If another party has filed an appeal, the parent's attorney should explain the appeals process to the parent and ensure that responsive papers are filed timely.

The appellate brief should be clear, concise, and comprehensive and also timely filed. The brief should reflect all relevant case law and present the best legal arguments available in state and federal law for the client's position. The brief should include novel legal arguments if there is a chance of developing favorable law in support of the parent's claim.

In jurisdictions in which a different attorney from the trial attorney handles the appeal, the trial attorney should take all steps necessary to facilitate appointing appellate counsel and work with the new attorney to identify appropriate issues for appeal. The attorney who handled the trial may have insight beyond what a new attorney could obtain by reading the trial transcript.

If appellate counsel differs from the trial attorney, the appellate attorney should meet with the client as soon as possible. At the initial meeting, appellate counsel should determine the client's position and goals in the appeal. Appellate counsel should not be bound by the determinations of the client's position and goals made by trial counsel and should independently determine his or her client's position and goals on appeal.

If oral arguments are scheduled, the attorney should be prepared, organized, and direct. Appellate counsel should inform the client of the date, time and place scheduled for oral argument of the appeal upon receiving notice from the appellate court. Oral argument of the appeal on behalf of the client should not be waived, absent the express approval of the client, unless doing so would benefit the client. For example, in some jurisdictions appellate counsel may file a reply brief instead of oral argument. The attorney should weigh the pros and cons of each option.

Commentary

Appellate skills differ from the skills most trial attorneys use daily. The parent's attorney may wish to seek training on appellate practice and guidance from an experienced appellate advocate when drafting the brief and preparing for argument. An appeal can have a significant impact on the trial judge who heard the case and trial courts throughout the state, as well as the individual client and family.

43. Request an expedited appeal, when feasible, and file all necessary paperwork while the appeal is pending.

Action

If the state court allows, the attorney in a child welfare matter should always consider requesting an expedited appeal. In this request, the attorney should provide information about why the case should be expedited, such as any special characteristics about the child and why delay would harm the relationship between the parent and child.

44. Communicate the results of the appeal and its implications to the client.

Action

The parent's attorney should communicate the result of the appeal and its implications, and provide the client with a copy of the appellate decision. If, as a result of the appeal, the attorney needs to file any motions with the trial court, the attorney should do so.

OBLIGATIONS OF ATTORNEY MANAGERS[20]

Attorney Managers are urged to:

1. Clarify attorney roles and expectations.

Action

The attorney manager must ensure that staff attorneys understand their role in representing clients and the expectations of the attorney manager concerning all staff duties. In addition to in-office obligations staff attorneys may attend meetings, conferences, and trainings. The attorney may need to attend child welfare agency or service provider meetings with clients. The manager should articulate these duties at the beginning of and consistently during the attorney's employment. The manager should emphasize the attorney's duties toward the client, and obligations to comply with practice standards.

Commentary

All employees want to know what is expected of them; one can only do a high-quality job when the person knows the parameters and expectations of the position. Therefore, the attorney manager must consistently inform staff of those expectations. Otherwise, the staff attorney is set up to fail. The work of representing parents is too important, and too difficult, to be handled by people who do not understand their role and lack clear expectations. These attorneys need the full support of supervisors and attorney managers to perform their highest quality work.

2. Determine and set reasonable caseloads for attorneys.[21]

Action

An attorney manager should determine reasonable caseloads for parents' attorneys and monitor them to ensure the maximum is not exceeded. Consider a caseload/workload study, review written materials about such studies, or look into caseload sizes in similar counties to accurately determine ideal attorney caseloads. When assessing the appropriate number of cases, remember to account for all attorney obligations, case difficulty, time required to prepare a case thoroughly, support staff assistance, travel time, experience level of attorneys, and available time (excluding vacation, holidays, sick leave, training and other non-case-related activity). If the attorney manager carries a case-load, the number of cases should reflect the time the individual spends on management duties.

Commentary
High caseload is considered a major barrier to quality representation and a source of high attorney turnover. It is essential to decide what a reasonable caseload is in your jurisdiction. How attorneys define cases and attorney obligations vary from place-to-place, but having a manageable caseload is crucial. The standards drafting committee recommended a caseload of no more than 50–100 cases depending on what the attorney can handle competently and fulfill these standards. The type of practice the attorney has, e.g., whether the attorney is part of a multidisciplinary representation team also has an impact on the appropriate caseload size. It is part of the attorney manager's job to advocate for adequate funding and to alert individuals in positions of authority when attorneys are regularly asked to take caseloads that exceed local standards.

3. Advocate for competitive salaries for staff attorneys.

Action
Attorney managers should advocate for attorney salaries that are competitive with other government and court appointed attorneys in the jurisdiction. To recruit and retain experienced attorneys, salaries must compare favorably with similarly situated attorneys.

Commentary
While resources are scarce, parents' attorneys deserve to be paid a competitive wage. They will likely not stay in their position nor be motivated to work hard without a reasonable salary. High attorney turnover may decrease when attorneys are paid well. Parents' rights to effective assistance of counsel may be compromised if parents' attorneys are not adequately compensated.

4. Develop a system for the continuity of representation.

Action
The attorney manager should develop a case assignment system that fosters ownership and involvement in the case by the parent's attorney.

The office can have a one-attorney: one-case (vertical representation) policy in which an attorney follows the case from initial filing through permanency and handles all aspects of the case. Alternatively, the cases may be assigned to a group of attorneys who handle all aspects of a case as a team and are all assigned to one judge. If a team approach is adopted, it is critical to establish mechanisms to aid communication about cases and promote accountability.

The attorney manager should also hire social workers, paralegals and/or parent advocates (parents familiar with the child welfare system because they were involved in the system and successfully reunited with their child), who should be "teamed" with the attorneys. These individuals can assist the attorney or attorney team with helping clients access services and information between hearings, and help the attorney organize and monitor the case.

Commentary

Parents' attorneys can provide the best representation for the client when they know a case and are invested in its outcome. Continuity of representation is critical for attorneys and parents to develop the trust that is essential to high quality representation. Additionally, having attorneys who are assigned to particular cases decreases delays because the attorney does not need to learn the case each time it is scheduled for court, but rather has extensive knowledge of the case history. The attorney also has the opportunity to monitor action on the case between court hearings. This system also makes it easier for the attorney manager to track how cases are handled. Whatever system is adopted, the manager must be clear about which attorney has responsibility for the case preparation, monitoring, and advocacy required throughout the case.

5. Provide attorneys with training and education opportunities regarding the special issues that arise in the client population.

Action

The attorney manager must ensure that each attorney has opportunities to participate in training and education programs. When a new attorney is hired, the attorney manager should assess that attorney's level of experience and readiness to handle cases. The attorney manager should develop an internal training program that pairs the new attorney with an experienced "attorney mentor." The new attorney should be required to: 1) observe each type of court proceeding (and mediation if available in the jurisdiction), 2) second-chair each type of proceeding, 3) try each type of case with the mentor second-chairing, and 4) try each type of proceeding on his or her own, with the mentor available to assist, before the attorney can begin handling cases alone.

Additionally, each attorney should attend at least 20 hours of relevant training before beginning, and at least15 hours of relevant training every year after. Training should include general legal topics such as evidence and trial skills, and child welfare-specific topics that are related to the client population the office is representing, such as:

- Relevant state, federal and case law, procedures and rules
- Available community resources
- State and federal benefit programs affecting parties in the child welfare system (e.g., SSI, SSA, Medicaid, UCCJEA)
- Federal Indian Law including the Indian Child Welfare Act and state law related to Native Americans
- Understanding mental illness
- Substance abuse issues (including assessment, treatment alternatives, confidentiality, impact of different drugs)
- Legal permanency options
- Reasonable efforts
- Termination of parental rights law
- Child development
- Legal ethics related to parent representation
- Negotiation strategies and techniques
- Protection orders/how domestic violence impacts parties in the child welfare system
- Appellate advocacy
- Immigration law in child welfare cases
- Education law in child welfare cases
- Basic principles of attachment theory
- Sexual abuse
- Dynamics of physical abuse and neglect
  - Shaken Baby Syndrome
  - Broken bones
  - Burns
  - Failure to Thrive
  - Munchausen's Syndrome by Proxy
- Domestic relations law

Commentary
Parents' attorneys should be encouraged to learn as much as possible and participate in conferences and trainings to expand their understanding of child welfare developments. While parents' attorneys often

lack extra time to attend conferences, the knowledge they gain will be invaluable. The philosophy of the office should stress the need for ongoing learning and professional growth. The attorney manager should require the attorneys to attend an achievable number of hours of training that will match the training needs of the attorneys. The court and Court Improvement Program[22] may be able to defray costs of attorney training or may sponsor multidisciplinary training that parents' attorneys should be encouraged to attend. Similarly, state and local bar associations, area law schools or local Child Law Institutes may offer education opportunities. Attorneys should have access to professional publications to stay current on the law and promising practices in child welfare. Child welfare attorneys benefit from the ability to strategize and share information and experiences with each other. Managers should foster opportunities for attorneys to support each other, discuss cases, and brainstorm regarding systemic issues and solutions.

6. Establish a regular supervision schedule.

Action
Attorney managers should ensure that staff attorneys meet regularly (at least once every two weeks) with supervising attorneys to discuss individual cases as well as any issues the attorney is encountering with the court, child welfare agency, service providers or others. The supervising attorney should help the staff attorney work through any difficulties the attorney is encountering in managing a caseload. Supervising attorneys should regularly observe the staff attorneys in court and be prepared to offer constructive criticism as needed. The supervising attorney should create an atmosphere in which the staff attorney is comfortable asking for help and sharing ideas.

Commentary
Parents' attorneys function best when they can learn, feel supported, and manage their cases with the understanding that their supervisors will assist as needed. By creating this office environment, the attorney manager invests in training high quality attorneys and results in long-term retention. Strong supervision helps attorneys avoid the burnout that could accompany the stressful work of representing parents in child welfare cases.

7. Create a brief and forms bank.

Action
Develop standard briefs, memoranda of law and forms that attorneys can use, so they do not "reinvent the wheel" for each new project. For

example, there could be sample discovery request forms, motions, notices of appeal, and petitions. Similarly, memoranda of law and appellate briefs follow patterns that the attorneys could use, although these should always be tailored to the specific case. These forms and briefs should be available on the computer and in hard copy and should be centrally maintained. They should also be well indexed for accessibility and updated as needed.

8. **Ensure the office has quality technical and support staff as well as adequate equipment, library materials, and computer programs to support its operations.**

Action
The attorney manager should advocate for high quality technical and staff support. The office should employ qualified legal assistants or paralegals and administrative assistants to help the attorneys. The attorney manager should create detailed job descriptions for these staff members to ensure they are providing necessary assistance. For instance, a qualified legal assistant can help: research, draft petitions, schedule and prepare witnesses and more.

The attorney manager should ensure attorneys have access to working equipment, a user-friendly library conducive to research, and computer programs for word processing, conducting research (Westlaw or Lexis/Nexis), caseload and calendar management, Internet access, and other supports that make the attorney's job easier and enhances client representation.

Commentary
By employing qualified staff, the attorneys will be free to perform tasks essential to quality representation. The attorneys must at least have access to a good quality computer, voice mail, fax machine, and copier to get the work done efficiently and with as little stress as possible

9. **Develop and follow a recruiting and hiring practice focused on hiring highly qualified candidates.**

Action
The attorney manager should hire the best attorneys possible. The attorney manager should form a hiring committee made up of managing and line attorneys and possibly a client or former client of the office. Desired qualities of a new attorney should be determined, focusing on educational and professional achievements; experience and commitment to representing parents and to the child welfare field; interpersonal skills; diversity and the needs of the office; writing and

verbal skills; second language skills; and ability to handle pressure. Widely advertising the position will draw a wider candidate pool. The hiring committee should set clear criteria for screening candidates before interviews and should conduct thorough interviews and post-interview discussions to choose the candidate with the best skills and strongest commitment. Reference checks should be completed before extending an offer.

Commentary
Hiring high quality attorneys raises the level of representation and the level of services parents in the jurisdiction receive. The parent attorney's job is complicated and stressful. There are many tasks to complete in a short time. It is often difficult to connect with, build trust and represent the parent. New attorneys must be aware of these challenges and be willing and able to overcome them. Efforts should be made to recruit staff who reflect the racial, ethnic, and cultural backgrounds of the clients. It is particularly important to have staff who can communicate with the clients in their first languages, whenever possible.

10. Develop and implement an attorney evaluation process.

Action
The attorney manager should develop an evaluation system that focuses on consistency, constructive criticism, and improvement. Some factors to evaluate include: communicating with the client, preparation and trial skills, working with clients and other professionals, complying with practice standards, and ability to work within a team. During the evaluation process, the attorney manager should consider:

- observing the attorney in court;
- reviewing the attorney's files;
- talking with colleagues and clients, when appropriate, about the attorney's performance;
- having the attorney fill out a self-evaluation; and
- meeting in person with the attorney.

Where areas of concern are noted, the evaluation process should identify and document specific steps to address areas needing improvement.

Commentary
A solid attorney evaluation process helps attorneys know what they should be working on, management's priorities, their strengths and

areas for improvement. A positive process supports attorneys in their positions, empowers them to improve and reduces burnout.

11. Work actively with other stakeholders to improve the child welfare system, including court procedures.

Action
The attorney manager should participate, or designate someone from the staff to participate, in multidisciplinary committees within the jurisdiction that are focused on improving the local child welfare system. Examples of such committees include: addressing issues of disproportional representation of minorities in foster care, improving services for incarcerated parents, allowing parents pre-petition representation, drafting court rules and procedures, drafting protocols about outreach to missing parents and relatives, removing permanency barriers and delays, and accessing community-based services for parents and children. Similarly, the attorney manager should participate in, and strongly encourage staff participation in, multidisciplinary training.

Commentary
Working on systemic change with all stakeholders in the jurisdiction is one way to serve the parents the office represents as well as their children. Active participation of parents' attorneys ensures that projects and procedures are equitably developed, protect parents' interests, and the attorneys are more likely to work on them over the long term. Collaboration can, and generally does, benefit all stakeholders.

ROLE OF THE COURT

The court is urged to:

1. Recognize the importance of the parent attorney's role.

Commentary
The judge sets the tone in the courtroom. Therefore, it is very important that the judge respects all parties, including the parents and parents' counsel. Representing parents is difficult and emotional work, but essential to ensuring justice is delivered in child abuse and neglect cases. When competent attorneys advocate for parent clients, the judge's job becomes easier. The judge is assured that the parties are presenting all relevant evidence, and the judge can make a well-reasoned decision that protects the parents' rights. Also, by respecting and understanding the parent attorney's role, the judge sets an example for others.

2. Establish uniform standards of representation for parents' attorneys.

Commentary

By establishing uniform representation rules or standards, the judge can put the parents' attorneys in the jurisdiction on notice that a certain level of representation will be required for the attorney to continue to receive appointments. The rules or standards should be jurisdiction specific, but should include the elements of these standards.

3. Ensure the attorneys who are appointed to represent parents in abuse and neglect cases are qualified, well-trained, and held accountable for practice that complies with these standards.

Commentary

Once the standards are established, the court must hold all parents' attorneys accountable to them. A system should be developed that would delineate when an attorney would be removed from a case for failure to comply with the standards, and what actions, or inactions, would result in the attorney's removal from the appointment list (or a court recommendation to an attorney manager that an attorney be disciplined within the parent attorney office). The court should encourage attorneys to participate in educational opportunities, and the judge should not appoint attorneys who have failed to meet the minimum annual training requirements set out in the rules or standards.

4. Ensure appointments are made when a case first comes before the court, or before the first hearing, and last until the case has been dismissed from the court's jurisdiction.

Commentary

The parent is disadvantaged in a child abuse and neglect case if not represented by a competent attorney throughout the life of the case. The attorney can explain the case to the parent, counsel the parent on how best to achieve the parent's goals with respect to the child, and assist the parent access necessary services. In most child welfare cases, the parent cannot afford an attorney and requires the court to appoint one. The court should make every effort to obtain an attorney for that parent as early in the case as feasible – preferably before the case comes to court for the first time or at the first hearing. In jurisdictions in which parents only obtain counsel for the termination of parental rights hearing, the parent has little chance of prevailing. A family that may have been reunified if the parent had appropriate legal support is separated forever.

5. Ensure parents' attorneys receive fair compensation.

Commentary
While resources are scarce, parents' attorneys deserve a competitive wage. They should receive the same wage as other government and court-appointed attorneys for other parties in the child abuse and neglect case. Parents' rights to effective assistance of counsel may be compromised if parents' attorneys are not adequately compensated. In most jurisdictions, the court sets the attorneys' fees and individual judges can recommend to court administration that parents' attorneys should be well compensated.

6. Ensure timely payment of fees and costs for attorneys.

Commentary
Often judges must sign fee petitions and approve payment of costs for attorneys. The judges should do so promptly so parents' attorneys can focus on representing clients, not worrying about being paid.

7. Provide interpreters, investigators and other specialists needed by the attorneys to competently represent clients. Ensure attorneys are reimbursed for supporting costs, such as use of experts, investigation services, interpreters, etc.

Commentary
Attorneys can not provide competent representation for parents without using certain specialists. For instance, if the client speaks a language different from the attorney, the attorney must have access to interpreters for attorney/client meetings. Interpreter costs should not be deducted from the attorney's compensation. A parent should be permitted to use an expert of the parent's choosing in some contested cases. If the expert charges a fee, the court should reimburse that fee separate and apart from what the court is paying the attorney.

8. Ensure that attorneys who are receiving appointments carry a reasonable caseload that would allow them to provide competent representation for each of their clients.

Commentary
The maximum allowable caseload should be included in local standards of practice for parents' attorneys. This committee recommends no more than 50–100 cases for full time attorneys, depending on the type of practice the attorney has and whether the attorney is able to provide each client with representation that follows these standards. Once this number has been established, the court should not appoint an attorney to cases once the attorney has reached the maximum level.

Attorneys can only do high quality work for a limited number of clients, and each client deserves the attorney's full attention. Of course, the caseload decision is closely tied to adequate compensation. If paid appropriately, the attorney will have less incentive to overextend and accept a large number of cases.

9. **Ensure all parties, including the parent's attorney, receive copies of court orders and other documentation.**

Commentary
The court should have a system to ensure all parties receive necessary documentation in a timely manner. If the parent and parent attorney do not have the final court order, they do not know what is expected of them and of the other parties. If the child welfare agency, for example, is ordered to provide the parent with a certain service within two weeks, the parent's attorney must know that. After two weeks, if the service has not been provided, the attorney will want to follow up with the court. In some jurisdictions, copies of court orders are handed to each party before they leave the courtroom. This is an ideal situation, and if it is not feasible, the court should determine what other distribution method will work.

10. **Provide contact information between clients and attorneys.**

Commentary
Often parties in child welfare cases are difficult to locate or contact. Some parents lack telephones. The court can help promote contact between the attorney and parent by providing contact information to both individuals.

11. **Ensure child welfare cases are heard promptly with a view towards timely decision making and thorough review of issues.**

Commentary
Judges should attempt to schedule hearings and make decisions quickly. Allotted court time should be long enough for the judge to thoroughly review the case and conduct a meaningful hearing.

When possible, judges should schedule hearings for times certain to avoid delaying attorneys unnecessarily in court. When attorneys are asked to wait through the rest of the morning calendar for one brief review hearing, limited dollars are spent to keep the attorney waiting in hallways, rather than completing an independent investigation, or researching alternative placement or treatment options.

Judges should avoid delays in decision making. Delays in decision making can impact visitation, reunification and even emotional closure when needed. If a parent does not know what the judge expects, the parent may lack direction or motivation to engage in services.

ACKNOWLEDGMENTS

These standards were drafted by Mimi Laver, Legal Education Director, ABA Center on Children and the Law, with the input of the following individuals:

Valerie Adelson, Staff Director, ABA Standing Committee on Substance Abuse, Chicago, IL

Kris Berliant, ABA Judicial Division Staff, Chicago, IL,

Sharon Biasca, Managing Attorney, Juvenile Court Project, Pittsburgh, PA

Terry Brooks, Staff Director, ABA Standing Committee on Legal Aid and Indigent Defendants, Chicago, IL

Joanne Brown, Consultant, ABA Center on Children and the Law, Washington, DC

Shante Bullock, Program Administrator, ABA Center on Children and the Law, Washington, DC

Kate Chester, Director, Family Preservation Law Center, Siler City, NC

Claire Chiamulera, Communications Manager/Legal Editor, ABA Center on Children and the Law, Washington, DC

Andy Cohen, Staff Counsel, Children and Family Program, Committee for Public Counsel Services, Boston, MA

Emily Cooke, Special Assistant for Court Improvement, Children's Bureau, Washington, DC

Howard Davidson, Director, ABA Center on Children and the Law, Washington, DC

Alicia Davis, Family Issues Unit Supervisor, Division of Planning and Analysis, Colorado State Court Administrator's Office, Denver, CO

Amanda Donnelly, Staff Attorney, National Association of Counsel for Children, Denver, CO

Patsy Engelhard, Staff Director, ABA Litigation Division, Chicago, IL

Debby Freedman, Director, Family Advocacy Unit, Community Legal Services, Philadelphia, PA

Chris Gottlieb, Co-Director, NYU Family Defense Clinic, New York, NY

Judge Ernestine Gray, Orleans Parish Juvenile Court, Representative, ABA Judicial Division, New Orleans, LA

Bill Grimm, Senior Attorney, Child Welfare/Foster Care, National Center for Youth Law, Oakland, CA

Ann Haralambie, Representative for ABA Family Law Division, Tucson, AZ

Mark Hardin, Director, Child Welfare, ABA Center on Children and Law, Washington, DC

Sue Jacobs, Executive Director, Center for Family Representation, New York, NY

Judge William Jones, Consultant, ABA Center on Children and the Law, Charlotte, NC

Candice Maze, Representative, ABA Steering Committee on the Unmet Legal Needs of Children, Miami, FL

Moreen Murphy, Staff Director, ABA Steering Committee on the Unmet Legal Needs of Children

Joanne Moore, WA State Office of Public Defense, Olympia, WA

Christina Plum, ABA Young Lawyer's Division Chair, PO Box 11756, Milwaukee, WI

Jennifer Renne, Assistant Director, Child Welfare, ABA Center on Children and the Law, Washington, DC

Professor Catherine J. Ross, George Washington University Law School, Representative for ABA Individual Rights and Responsibilities Section, Washington, DC

Don Saunders, Director, Civil Legal Services, National Legal Aid and Defender Association, Washington, DC

Tanya Terrell-Collier, Staff Director, ABA Individual Rights and Responsibilities Section, Washington, DC

Marvin Ventrell, Executive Director, National Association of Counsel for Children, Denver, CO

Mary Walker, Nashville, TN

Judge Joyce Warren, Tenth Division Circuit Court, Little Rock, AR

Sylvia Young, Washington, DC

Their input was essential to this project, and their willingness to assist was extraordinary.

NOTES

1. Model Rules of Professional Conduct 1.1 (Competence).
2. The National Association of Counsel for Children is accredited by the American Bar Association to certify attorneys as specialists in Child Welfare Law. The Certification Program is open to attorneys who represent children, parents, or agencies in child welfare proceedings.
3. Model Rule 1.3 (Diligence).
4. Model Rule 1.4 (Communication).
5. Model Rule 2.1 (Advisor).
6. Model Rule 1.2 (Scope of Representation and Allocation of Authority).
7. Model Rule 1.6 (Confidentiality of Information).
8. Model Rule 1.4 (Communication).
9. *Id.*
10. *Id.*
11. Model Rules 1.7 (Conflict of Interest: Current Client); 1.8 (Conflict of Interest: Current Clients: Specific Rules); 1.9 (Duties to Former Clients).
12. Renne, Jennifer L. Chapter 4, page 49, "Handling Conflicts of Interest," *Legal Ethics in Child Welfare Cases.* Washington, DC: American Bar Association, 2004.
13. Model Rule 1.3 (Diligence).
14. Model Rules 1.1 (Competence); 1.3 (Diligence).
15. Model Rule 1.4 (Communication).
16. Model Rules 1.1 (Competence); 1.3 (Diligence).
17. *Id.*
18. *Id.*
19. Model Rule 3.1 (Meritorious Claims and Contentions).
20. Model Rule 5.1 (Responsibility of Partners, Managers and Supervisory Lawyers).
21. Model Rule 1.1 (Competence).
22. The Court Improvement Program (CIP) is a federal grant to each state's (as well as the District of Columbia and Puerto Rico) supreme court. The funds must be used to improve child abuse and neglect courts. States vary in how they allocate the dollars, but funds are often used for training, benchbooks, pilot projects, model courts and information technology systems for the courts.

Model Act Governing the Representation of Children in Abuse, Neglect, and Dependency Proceedings[1]

AUGUST 2011

SECTION 1. DEFINITIONS

In this [act]:

(a) "Abuse and neglect proceeding" means a court proceeding under [cite state statute] for protection of a child from abuse or neglect or a court proceeding under [cite state statute] in which termination of parental rights is at issue.[2] These proceedings include:
   (1) abuse;
   (2) neglect;
   (3) dependency;
   (4) child in voluntary placement in state care;
   (5) termination of parental rights;
   (6) permanency hearings; and
   (7) post termination of parental rights through adoption or other permanency proceeding.

(b) A child is:
   (1) an individual under the age of 18; or
   (2) an individual under the age of 22 who remains under the jurisdiction of the juvenile court.

(c) "Child's lawyer" (or "lawyer for children") means a lawyer who provides legal services for a child and who owes the same duties, including undivided loyalty, confidentiality and competent representation, to the child as is due an adult client, subject to Section 7 of this Act.[3]

(d) "Best interest advocate" means an individual, not functioning or intended to function as the child's lawyer, appointed by the court to assist the court in determining the best interests of the child.

(e) "Developmental level" is a measure of the ability to communicate and understand others, taking into account such factors as age, mental capacity, level of education, cultural background, and degree of language acquisition.[4]

Legislative Note: States should implement a mechanism to bring children into court when they have been voluntarily placed into state care, if such procedures do not already exist. Court action should be triggered after a specific number of days in voluntary care (not fewer than 30 days, but not more than 90 days).

Commentary
Under the Act, a "child's lawyer" is a client-directed lawyer in a traditional attorney-client relationship with the child. A "best interests advocate" does not function as the child's lawyer and is not bound by the child's expressed wishes in determining what to advocate, although the best interests advocate should consider those wishes.

The best interest advocate may be a lawyer or a lay person, such as a court-appointed special advocate, or CASA. The best interests advocate assists the court in determining the best interests of a child and will therefore perform many of the functions formerly attributable to guardians *ad litem,* but best interests advocates are not to function as the child's lawyer. A lawyer appointed as a best interest advocate shall function as otherwise set forth in state law.

SECTION 2. APPLICABILITY AND RELATIONSHIP TO OTHER LAW

(f) This [act] applies to an abuse and neglect proceeding pending or commenced on or after [the effective date of this act].

(g) The child in these proceedings is a party.

SECTION 3. APPOINTMENT IN ABUSE OR NEGLECT PROCEEDING

(a) The court shall appoint a child's lawyer for each child who is the subject of a petition in an abuse and neglect proceeding. The appointment of a child's lawyer must be made as soon as practicable to ensure effective representation of the child and, in any event, before the first court hearing.

(b) In addition to the appointment of a child's lawyer, the court may appoint a best interest advocate to assist the court in determining the child's best interests.

(c) The court may appoint one child's lawyer to represent siblings if there is no conflict of interest as defined under the applicable rules of professional conduct.[5] The court may appoint additional counsel to represent individual siblings at a child's lawyer's request due to a conflict of interest between or among the siblings.

(d) The applicable rules of professional conduct and any law governing the obligations of lawyers to their clients shall apply to such appointed lawyers for children.

(e) The appointed child's lawyer shall represent the child at all stages of the proceedings, unless otherwise discharged by order of court.[6]

(f) A child's right to counsel may not be waived at any court proceeding.

Commentary
This act recognizes the right of every child to have quality legal representation and a voice in any abuse, neglect, dependency, or termination of parental rights proceeding, regardless of developmental level. Nothing in this Act precludes a child from retaining a lawyer. States should provide a lawyer to a child who has been placed into state custody through a voluntary placement arrangement. The fact that the child is in the state's custody through the parent's voluntary decision should not diminish the child's entitlement to a lawyer.

A best interest advocate does not replace the appointment of a lawyer for the child. A best interest advocate serves to provide guidance to the court with respect to the child's best interest and does not establish a lawyer-client relationship with the child. Nothing in this Act restricts a court's ability to appoint a best interest advocate in any proceeding. Because this Act deals specifically with lawyers for children, it will not further address the role of the best interest advocate.

The child is entitled to conflict-free representation and the applicable rules of professional conduct must be applied in the same manner as they would be applied for lawyers for adults. A lawyer representing siblings should maintain the same lawyer-client relationship with respect to each child.

SECTION 4. QUALIFICATIONS OF THE CHILD'S LAWYER

(a) The court shall appoint as the child's lawyer an individual who is qualified through training and experience, according to standards established by [insert reference to source of standards].

(b) Lawyers for children shall receive initial training and annual continuing legal education that is specific to child welfare law. Lawyers for children shall be familiar with all relevant federal, state, and local applicable laws.

(c) Lawyers for children shall not be appointed to new cases when their present caseload exceeds more than a reasonable number given the jurisdiction, the percent of the lawyer's practice spent on abuse and neglect cases, the complexity of the case, and other relevant factors.

Legislative Note: States that adopt training standards and standards of practice for children's lawyers should include the bracketed portion of this section and insert a reference to the state laws, court rules, or administrative guidelines containing those standards.[7]

Jurisdictions are urged to specify a case limit at the time of passage of this Act.

Commentary
States should establish minimum training requirements for lawyers who represent children. Such training should focus on applicable law, skills needed to develop a meaningful lawyer-client relationship with child-clients, techniques to assess capacity in children, as well as the many interdisciplinary issues that arise in child welfare cases.

The lawyer needs to spend enough time on each abuse and neglect case to establish a lawyer-client relationship and zealously advocate for the client. A lawyer's caseload must allow realistic performance of functions assigned to the lawyer under the [Act]. The amount of time and the number of children a lawyer can represent effectively will differ based on a number of factors, including type of case, the demands of the jurisdiction, whether the lawyer is affiliated with a children's law office, whether the lawyer is assisted by investigators or other child welfare professionals, and the percent of the lawyer's practice spent on abuse and neglect cases. States are encouraged to conduct caseload analyses to determine guidelines for lawyers representing children in abuse and neglect cases.

SECTION 5. ORDER OF APPOINTMENT

(a) Subject to subsection (b), an order of appointment of a child's lawyer shall be in writing and on the record, identify the lawyer who will act in that capacity, and clearly set forth the terms of the appointment, including the reasons for the appointment, rights of access as provided under Section 8, and applicable terms of compensation as provided under Section 12.

(b) In an order of appointment issued under subsection (a), the court may identify a private organization, law school clinical program or governmental program through which a child's lawyer will be provided. The organization or program shall designate the lawyer who will act in that capacity and notify the parties and the court of the name of the assigned lawyer as soon as practicable.[8] Additionally, the organization or program shall notify the parties and the court of any changes in the individual assignment.

SECTION 6. DURATION OF APPOINTMENT

Unless otherwise provided by a court order, an appointment of a child's lawyer in an abuse and neglect proceeding continues in effect until the lawyer is discharged by court order or the case is dismissed.[9] The appointment includes all stages thereof, from removal from the home or initial appointment through all available appellate proceedings. With the permission of the court, the lawyer may arrange for supplemental or separate counsel to handle proceedings at an appellate stage.[10]

Commentary

As long as the child remains in state custody, even if the state custody is long-term or permanent, the child should retain the right to counsel so that the child's lawyer can deal with the issues that may arise while the child is in custody but the case is not before the court.

SECTION 7. DUTIES OF CHILD'S LAWYER AND SCOPE OF REPRESENTATION

(a) A child's lawyer shall participate in any proceeding concerning the child with the same rights and obligations as any other lawyer for a party to the proceeding.

(b) The duties of a child's lawyer include, but are not limited to:
  (1) taking all steps reasonably necessary to represent the client in the proceeding, including but not limited to: interviewing and counseling the client, preparing a case theory and strategy, preparing for and participating in negotiations and hearings, drafting and submitting motions, memoranda and orders, and such other steps as established by the applicable standards of practice for lawyers acting on behalf of children in this jurisdiction;
  (2) reviewing and accepting or declining, after consultation with the client, any proposed stipulation for an order affecting the child and explaining to the court the basis for any opposition;
  (3) taking action the lawyer considers appropriate to expedite the proceeding and the resolution of contested issues;
  (4) where appropriate, after consultation with the client, discussing the possibility of settlement or the use of alternative forms of dispute resolution and participating in such processes to the extent permitted under the law of this state;[11]
  (5) meeting with the child prior to each hearing and for at least one in-person meeting every quarter;
  (6) where appropriate and consistent with both confidentiality and the child's legal interests, consulting with the best interests advocate;

(7) prior to every hearing, investigating and taking necessary legal action regarding the child's medical, mental health, social, education, and overall well-being;

(8) visiting the home, residence, or any prospective residence of the child, including each time the placement is changed;

(9) seeking court orders or taking any other necessary steps in accordance with the child's direction to ensure that the child's health, mental health, educational, developmental, cultural and placement needs are met; and

(10) representing the child in all proceedings affecting the issues before the court, including hearings on appeal or referring the child's case to the appropriate appellate counsel as provided for by/mandated by [inset local rule/law etc].

Commentary

The national standards mentioned in (b)(1) include the *ABA Standards of Practice for Lawyers Who Represent Children in Abuse and Neglect Cases.*

In order to comply with the duties outlined in this section, lawyers must have caseloads that allow realistic performance of these functions.

The child's lawyer may request authority from the court to pursue issues on behalf of the child, administratively or judicially, even if those issues do not specifically arise from the court appointment.[12] Such ancillary matters include special education, school discipline hearings, mental health treatment, delinquency or criminal issues, status offender matters, guardianship, adoption, paternity, probate, immigration matters, medical care coverage, SSI eligibility, youth transitioning out of care issues, postsecondary education opportunity qualification, and tort actions for injury, as appropriate.[13] The lawyer should make every effort to ensure that the child is represented by legal counsel in all ancillary legal proceedings, either personally, when the lawyer is competent to do so, or through referral or collaboration. Having one lawyer represent the child across multiple proceedings is valuable because the lawyer is better able to understand and fully appreciate the various issues as they arise and how those issues may affect other proceedings.

(c) When the child is capable of directing the representation by expressing his or her objectives, the child's lawyer shall maintain a normal client-lawyer relationship with the child in accordance with the rules of professional conduct. In a developmentally appropriate manner, the lawyer shall elicit the child's wishes and advise the child as to options.

Commentary

The lawyer-client relationship for the child's lawyer is fundamentally indistinguishable from the lawyer-client relationship in any other situation and includes duties of client direction,[14] confidentiality,[15] diligence,[16] competence,[17] loyalty,[18] communication,[19] and the duty to provide independent advice.[20] Client direction requires the lawyer to abide by the client's decision about the objectives of the representation. In order for the child to have an independent voice in abuse and neglect proceedings, the lawyer shall advocate for the child's counseled and expressed wishes.[21] Moreover, providing the child with an independent and client-directed lawyer ensures that the child's legal rights and interests are adequately protected.

The child's lawyer needs to explain his or her role to the client and, if applicable, explain in what strictly limited circumstances the lawyer cannot advocate for the client's expressed wishes and in what circumstances the lawyer may be required to reveal confidential information. This explanation should occur during the first meeting so the client understands the terms of the relationship.

In addition to explaining the role of the child's lawyer, the lawyer should explain the legal process to the child in a developmentally appropriate manner as required by Rule 1.4 of the ABA Model Rules of Professional Conduct or its equivalent.[22] This explanation can and will change based on age, cognitive ability, and emotional maturity of the child. The lawyer needs to take the time to explain thoroughly and in a way that allows and encourages the child to ask questions and that ensures the child's understanding. The lawyer should also facilitate the child's participation in the proceeding (See Section 9).

In order to determine the objectives of the representation of the child, the child's lawyer should develop a relationship with the client. The lawyer should achieve a thorough knowledge of the child's circumstances and needs. The lawyer should visit the child in the child's home, school, or other appropriate place where the child is comfortable. The lawyer should observe the child's interactions with parents, foster parents, and other caregivers. The lawyer should maintain regular and ongoing contact with the child throughout the case.

The child's lawyer helps to make the child's wishes and voice heard but is not merely the child's mouthpiece. As with any lawyer, a child's lawyer is both an advocate and a counselor for the client. Without unduly influencing the child, the lawyer should advise the child by providing options and information to assist the child in making decisions. The lawyer should explain the practical effects of taking various positions, the likelihood that a court will accept particular arguments, and the impact of such decisions on the child, other family members, and future legal proceedings.[23] The lawyer should investigate the relevant facts, interview persons with significant knowledge of the child's history, review relevant records, and work with others in the case.

(d) The child's lawyer shall determine whether the child has diminished capacity pursuant to the Model Rules of Professional Conduct. {STATES MAY CONSIDER INSERTING THE FOLLOWING TWO SENTENCES:} [Under this subsection a child shall be presumed to be capable of directing representation at the age of ___. The presumption of diminished capacity is rebutted if, in the sole discretion of the lawyer, the child is deemed capable of directing representation.] In making the determination, the lawyer should consult the child and may consult other individuals or entities that can provide the child's lawyer with the information and assistance necessary to determine the child's ability to direct the representation.

When a child client has diminished capacity, the child's lawyer shall make a good faith effort to determine the child's needs and wishes. The lawyer shall, as far as reasonably possible, maintain a normal client-lawyer relationship with the client and fulfill the duties as outlined in Section 7(b) of this Act. During a temporary period or on a particular issue where a normal client-lawyer relationship is not reasonably possible to maintain, the child's lawyer shall make a substituted judgment determination. A substituted judgment determination includes determining what the child would decide if he or she were capable of making an adequately considered decision, and representing the child in accordance with that determination. The lawyer should take direction from the child as the child develops the capacity to direct the lawyer. The lawyer shall advise the court of the determination of capacity and any subsequent change in that determination.

Commentary
A determination of incapacity may be incremental and issue-specific, thus enabling the child's lawyer to continue to function as a client-directed lawyer as to major questions in the proceeding. Determination of diminished capacity requires ongoing re-assessment. A child may be able to direct the lawyer with respect to a particular issue at one time but not another. Similarly, a child may be able to determine some

positions in the case, but not others. For guidance in assessing diminished capacity, see the commentary to Section (e). The lawyer shall advise the court of the determination of capacity and any subsequent change in that determination.

In making a substituted judgment determination, the child's lawyer may wish to seek guidance from appropriate professionals and others with knowledge of the child, including the advice of an expert. A substituted judgment determination is not the same as determining the child's best interests; determination of a child's best interests remains solely the province of the court. Rather, it involves determining what the child would decide if he or she were able to make an adequately considered decision.[24] A lawyer should determine the child's position based on objective facts and information, not personal beliefs. To assess the needs and interests of this child, the lawyer should observe the child in his or her environment, and consult with experts.[25]

In formulating a substituted judgment position, the child's lawyer's advocacy should be child-centered, research-informed, permanency-driven, and holistic.[26] The child's needs and interests, not the adults' or professionals' interests, must be the center of all advocacy. For example, lawyers representing very young children must truly *see* the world through the child's eyes and formulate their approach from that perspective, gathering information and gaining insight into the child's experiences to inform advocacy related to placement, services, treatment and permanency.[27] The child's lawyer should be proactive and seek out opportunities to observe and interact with the very young child client. It is also essential that lawyers for very young children have a firm working knowledge of child development and special entitlements for children under age five.[28]

When determining a substituted judgment position, the lawyer shall take into consideration the child's legal interests based on objective criteria as set forth in the laws applicable to the proceeding, the goal of expeditious resolution of the case and the use of the least restrictive or detrimental alternatives available. The child's lawyer should seek to speed the legal process, while also maintaining the child's critical relationships.

The child's lawyer should not confuse inability to express a preference with unwillingness to express a preference. If an otherwise competent child chooses not to express a preference on a particular matter, the child's lawyer should determine if the child wishes the lawyer to take no position in the proceeding, or if the child wishes the lawyer or someone else to make the decision for him or her. In either case, the lawyer is bound to follow the client's direction. A child may be able to direct the lawyer with respect to a particular issue at one time but not at another. A child may be able to determine some positions in the case but not others.

(e) When the child's lawyer reasonably believes that the client has diminished capacity, is at risk of substantial physical, financial or other harm unless action is taken, and cannot adequately act in the client's own interest, the lawyer may take reasonably necessary protective action, including consulting with individuals or entities that have the ability to take action to protect the client and, in appropriate cases, seeking the appointment of a best interest advocate or investigator to make an independent recommendation to the court with respect to the best interests of the child.

When taking protective action, the lawyer is impliedly authorized under Model Rule 1.6(a) to reveal information about the child, but only to the extent reasonably necessary to protect the child's interests.[29] Information relating to the representation of a child with diminished capacity is protected by Rule 1.6 and Rule 1.14 of the ABA Model Rules of Professional Conduct. [OR ENTER STATE RULE CITATION]

Commentary
Consistent with Rule 1.14, ABA Model Rules of Professional Conduct (2004), the child's lawyer should determine whether the child has sufficient maturity to understand and form an attorney-client relationship and whether the child is capable of making reasoned judgments and engaging in meaningful communication. It is the responsibility of the child's lawyer to determine whether the child suffers from diminished capacity. This decision shall be made after sufficient contact and regular communication with the client. Determination about capacity should be grounded in insights from child development science and should focus on the child's decision-making process rather than the child's choices themselves. Lawyers should be careful not to conclude that the child suffers diminished capacity from a client's insistence upon a course of action that the lawyer considers unwise or at variance with lawyer's view.[30]

When determining the child's capacity the lawyer should elicit the child's expressed wishes in a developmentally appropriate manner. The lawyer should not expect the child to convey information in the same way as an adult client. A child's age is not determinative of diminished capacity. For example, even very young children are regarded as having opinions that are entitled to weight in legal proceedings concerning their custody.[31]

Criteria for determining diminished capacity include the child's developmental stage, cognitive ability, emotional and mental development, ability to communicate, ability to understand consequences, consistency of the child's decisions, strength of wishes and the opinions of others, including social workers, therapists, teachers, family members or a hired expert.[32] To assist in the assessment, the lawyer should ask questions in developmentally appropriate language to determine whether the child understands the nature and purpose of the proceeding and the risks and benefits of a desired position.[33] A child may have the ability to make certain decisions, but not others. A child with diminished capacity often has the ability to understand, deliberate upon, and reach conclusions about matters affecting the child's own well-being such as sibling visits, kinship visits, and school choice and should continue to direct counsel in those areas in which he or she does have capacity. The lawyer should continue to assess the child's capacity as it may change over time.

When the lawyer determines that the child has diminished capacity, the child is at risk of substantial harm, the child cannot adequately act in his or her own interest, and the use of the lawyer's counseling role is unsuccessful, the lawyer may take protective action. Substantial harm includes physical, sexual and psychological harm. Protective action includes consultation with family members, or professionals who work with the child. Lawyers may also utilize a period of reconsideration to allow for an improvement or clarification of circumstances or to allow for an improvement in the child's capacity.[34] This rule reminds lawyers that, among other things, they should ultimately be guided by the wishes and values of the child to the extent they can be determined.[35]

"Information relating to the representation is protected by Model Rule 1.6. Therefore, unless authorized to do so, the lawyer may not disclose such information. When taking protective action pursuant to this section, the lawyer is impliedly authorized to make necessary disclosures, even when the client directs the lawyer to the contrary."[36] However the lawyer should make every effort to avoid disclosures if at all possible. Where disclosures are unavoidable, the lawyer must limit the disclosures as much as possible. Prior to any consultation, the lawyer should consider the impact on the client's position, and whether the individual is a party who might use the information to further his or her own interests. "At the very least, the lawyer should determine whether it is likely that the person or entity consulted with will act adversely to the client's interests before discussing matters related to the client."[37] If any disclosure by the lawyer will have a negative impact on the client's case or the lawyer-client relationship, the lawyer must consider whether representation can continue and whether the lawyer-client relationship can be re-established. "The lawyer's position in such cases is an unavoidably difficult one."[38]

A request made for the appointment of a best interest advocate to make an independent recommendation to the court with respect to the best interests of the child should be reserved for extreme cases, i.e. where the child is at risk of substantial physical harm, cannot act in his or her own interest and all protective action remedies have been exhausted. Requesting the judge to appoint a best interest advocate may undermine the relationship the lawyer has established with the child. It also potentially compromises confidential information the child may have revealed to the lawyer. The lawyer cannot ever become the best interest advocate, in part due to confidential information that the lawyer receives in the course of representation. Nothing in this section restricts a court from independently appointing a best interest advocate when it deems the appointment appropriate.

SECTION 8. ACCESS TO CHILD AND INFORMATION RELATING TO THE CHILD

(a) Subject to subsections (b) and (c), when the court appoints the child's lawyer, it shall issue an order, with notice to all parties, authorizing the child's lawyer to have access to:
   (1) the child; and
   (2) confidential information regarding the child, including the child's educational, medical, and mental health records, social services agency files, court records including court files involving allegations of abuse or neglect of the child, any delinquency records involving the child, and other information relevant to the issues in the proceeding, and reports that form the basis of any recommendation made to the court.

(b) A child's record that is privileged or confidential under law other than this [act] may be released to a child's lawyer appointed under this [act] only in accordance with that law, including any requirements in that law for notice and opportunity to object to release of records. Nothing in this act shall diminish or otherwise change the attorney-client privilege of the child, nor shall the child have any lesser rights than any other party in regard to this or any other evidentiary privilege. Information that is privileged under the lawyer-client relationship may not be disclosed except as otherwise permitted by law of this state other than this [act].

(c) An order issued pursuant to subsection (a) shall require that a child's lawyer maintain the confidentiality of information released pursuant to Model Rule 1.6. The court may impose any other condition or limitation on an order of access which is required by law, rules of professional conduct, the child's needs, or the circumstances of the proceeding.

(d) The custodian of any record regarding the child shall provide access to the record to an individual authorized access by order issued pursuant to subsection (a).

(e) Subject to subsection (b), an order issued pursuant to subsection (a) takes effect upon issuance.[39]

SECTION 9. PARTICIPATION IN PROCEEDINGS

(a) Each child who is the subject of an abuse and neglect proceeding has the right to attend and fully participate in all hearings related to his or her case.

(b) Each child shall receive notice from the child welfare agency worker and the child's lawyer of his or her right to attend the court hearings.

(c) If the child is not present at the hearing, the court shall determine whether the child was properly notified of his or her right to attend the hearing, whether the child wished to attend the hearing, whether the child had the means (transportation) to attend, and the reasons for the non-appearance.

(d) If the child wished to attend and was not transported to court the matter shall be continued.

(e) The child's presence shall only be excused after the lawyer for the child has consulted with the child and, with informed consent, the child has waived his or her right to attend.

(f) A child's lawyer appointed under this [act] is entitled to:
  (1) receive a copy of each pleading or other record filed with the court in the proceeding;
  (2) receive notice of and attend each hearing in the proceeding [and participate and receive copies of all records in any appeal that may be filed in the proceeding];
  (3) receive notice of and participate in any case staffing or case management conference regarding the child in an abuse and neglect proceeding; and
  (4) receive notice of any intent to change the child's placement. In the case of an emergency change, the lawyer shall receive notice as soon as possible but no later than 48 hours following the change of placement.

(g) A child's lawyer appointed under this [act] may not engage in ex parte contact with the court except as authorized by the applicable rules of professional conduct, court order, or other law.

(h) Subject to court approval, a party may call any best interest advocate as a witness for the purpose of cross-examination regarding the advocate's report, even if the advocate is not listed as a witness by a party.

(i) [In a jury trial, disclosure to the jury of the contents of a best interest advocate's report is subject to this state's rules of evidence.][40]

Commentary
Courts need to provide the child with notification of each hearing. The Court should enforce the child's right to attend and fully participate in all hearings related to his or her abuse and neglect proceeding.[41] Having the child in court emphasizes for the judge and all parties that this hearing is about the child. Factors to consider regarding the child's presence at court and participation in the proceedings include: whether the child wants to attend, the child's age, the child's developmental ability, the child's emotional maturity, the purpose of the hearing and whether the child would be severely traumatized by such attendance.

   Lawyers should consider the following options in determining how to provide the most meaningful experience for the child to participate: allowing the child to be present throughout the entire hearing, presenting the child's testimony in chambers adhering to all applicable rules of evidence, arranging for the child to visit the courtroom in advance, video or teleconferencing the child into the hearing, allowing the child to be present only when the child's input is required, excluding the child during harmful testimony, and presenting the child's statements in court adhering to all applicable rules of evidence.

Courts should reasonably accommodate the child to ensure the hearing is a meaningful experience for the child. The court should consider: scheduling hearing dates and times when the child is available and least likely to disrupt the child's routine, setting specific hearing times to prevent the child from having to wait, making courtroom waiting areas child friendly, and ensuring the child will be transported to and from each hearing.

The lawyer for the child plays an important role in the child's court participation. The lawyer shall ensure that the child is properly prepared for the hearing. The lawyer should meet the child in advance to let the child know what to expect at the hearing, who will be present, what their roles are, what will be discussed, and what decisions will be made. If the child would like to address the court, the lawyer should counsel with the child on what to say and how to say it. After the hearing, the lawyer should explain the judge's ruling and allow the child to ask questions about the proceeding.

Because of the wide range of roles assumed by best interest advocates in different jurisdictions, the question of whether a best interest advocate may be called as a witness should be left to the discretion of the court.

SECTION 10. LAWYER WORK PRODUCT AND TESTIMONY

(a) Except as authorized by [insert reference to this state's rules of professional conduct] or court rule, a child's lawyer may not:

(1) be compelled to produce work product developed during the appointment;

(2) be required to disclose the source of information obtained as a result of the appointment;

(3) introduce into evidence any report or analysis prepared by the child's lawyer; or

(4) provide any testimony that is subject to the attorney-client privilege or any other testimony unless ordered by the court.

Commentary

Nothing in this act shall diminish or otherwise change the lawyer-work product or attorney-client privilege protection for the child, nor shall the child have any lesser rights than any other party with respect to these protections.

If a state requires lawyers to report abuse or neglect under a mandated reporting statute, the state should list that statute under this section.

SECTION 11. CHILD'S RIGHT OF ACTION

(a) The child's lawyer may be liable for malpractice to the same extent as a lawyer for any other client.

(b) Only the child has a right of action for money damages against the child's lawyer for inaction or action taken in the capacity of child's lawyer.

SECTION 12. FEES AND EXPENSES IN ABUSE OR NEGLECT PROCEEDINGS

(a) In an abuse or neglect proceeding, a child's lawyer appointed pursuant to this [act] is entitled to reasonable and timely fees and expenses in an amount set by [court or state agency to be paid from (authorized public funds)].[42]

(b) To receive payment under this section, the payee shall complete and submit a written claim for payment, whether interim or final, justifying the fees and expenses charged.

(c) If after a hearing the court determines that a party whose conduct gave rise to a finding of abuse or neglect is able to defray all or part of the fees and expenses set pursuant to subsection (a), the court shall enter a judgment in favor of [the state, state agency, or political subdivision] against the party in an amount the court determines is reasonable.[43]

SECTION 13. EFFECTIVE DATE

This [act] takes effect on _____.

REPORT

> "The participation of counsel on behalf of **all** parties subject to juvenile and family court proceedings is essential to the administration of justice and to the fair and accurate resolution of issues at all stages of those proceedings." IJA/ABA, Juvenile Justice Standards, Standards Relating to Counsel for Private Parties, Std. 1.1, at 11 (1980) (emphasis added).

Courts in abuse and neglect cases dramatically shape a child's entire future in that the court decides where a child lives, with whom the child will live and whether the child's parental rights will be terminated. No other legal proceeding that pertains to children has such a major effect on their lives. While the outcome of an abuse and neglect case has drastic implications for both the parents and the children involved, only children's physical liberty is threatened. An abuse and neglect case that results in removal of the child from the home may immediately or ultimately result in the child being thrust into an array of confusing and frightening situations wherein the State moves the child from placement to placement with total strangers, puts the child in a group home, commits the child to an institution, or even locks the child up in detention for running away or otherwise violating a court order. Our notion of basic civil rights, and ABA Policy and Standards, demand that children and youth have a trained legal advocate to speak on their behalf and to protect their legal rights. There would be no question about legal representation for a child who was facing a month in juvenile detention, so why is there an issue for a child in an abuse and neglect case, where State intervention may last up to 18 years? The trauma faced by children in these proceedings has been recognized by at least one federal court which held that foster children have a constitutional right to adequate legal representation.[44]

Despite the gravity of these cases, the extent to which a child is entitled to legal representation varies not only from state to state, but from case to case, and all too often, from hearing to hearing. The root of these inconsistencies lies in the lack of a mandate for legal representation for children in abuse and neglect cases, and the lack of uniform standards for the legal representation of children, coupled with the lack of sufficient training necessary for attorneys to provide adequate representation to their child clients.

In 1996 the ABA adopted the *ABA Standards of Practice for Lawyers Who Represent Children in Abuse and Neglect Cases* (hereinafter "*ABA Abuse and Neglect Standards*") calling for a lawyer for every child subject to abuse and neglect proceedings.[45] The *ABA Abuse and Neglect Standards* state that "All children subject to court proceedings involving allegations of child abuse and neglect should have legal representation as long as the court jurisdiction continue." In 2005, the ABA unanimously passed policy that calls upon Congress, the States, and territories to ensure that "all dependent youth . . . be on equal footing with other parties in the dependency proceeding and have the right to quality legal representation, not simply an appointed lay guardian *ad litem* or lay volunteer advocate with no legal training, acting on their behalf in this court process."

The proposed *Model Act Governing the Representation of Children in Abuse, Neglect, and Dependency Proceedings* (hereinafter "Model Act") focuses on the representation of children in abuse and neglect cases to ensure that states have a model of ethical representation for children that is consistent with the *ABA Abuse and Neglect Standards*,[46] ABA Policy, and the ABA Model Rules of Professional Conduct (hereinafter "ABA Model Rules").

Although many states require that a lawyer be appointed for a child in an abuse and neglect proceeding, some require that the child's lawyer be "client directed" and others require the lawyer to act as a guardian *ad litem* whereby the attorney is charged with the duty of protecting and serving the "best interests" of the child. Often there is not "careful delineation of the distinctions between the ethical responsibilities of a lawyer to the client and the professional obligations of the lay guardian *ad litem* as a best interests witness for the court."[47] The states' use of different statutory language and mandated roles for child representation has led to much confusion within the field.

The proposed Model Act conforms to the clearly stated preference in the *ABA Abuse and Neglect Standards* for a client-directed lawyer for each child. Similarly, the proposed Model Act is consistent with the ABA Model Rules. The Model Act states that the child's lawyer should form an attorney-client relationship which is "fundamentally indistinguishable from the attorney-client relationship in any other situation and which includes duties of client direction, confidentiality, diligence, competence, loyalty, communication, and the duty to advise."[48]

Consonant with the ABA Model Rules, the drafters of the Model Act started from the premise that all child clients have the capacity to form an attorney–client relationship. An attorney must enter into representation of a child treating the child client as he or she would any other client to every extent possible. The attorney should give the child frank advice on what he or she thinks is the best legal remedy to achieve the child's expressed wishes. This decision should not be based on the attorney's mores or personal opinions; rather it should focus on the attorney's knowledge of the situation, the law, options available and the child's wishes. The proposed Model Act also provides specific guidance for lawyers charged with representing those child clients with diminished capacity. Some children (including infants, preverbal children, and children who are mentally or developmentally challenged) do not have the capacity to form a lawyer-client relationship. These child clients should be considered the exception, not the rule, and the structure of representation for children as a whole should be based upon a theory of competence and capacity.

Providing children in abuse and neglect cases with a client-directed 'traditional' lawyer is consistent with the thinking of national children's law experts. A conference on the representation of children was held at Fordham Law School in 1995 entitled *Ethical Issues in the Legal Representation of Children.* The conference examined the principles set out in the then-proposed (later adopted) *ABA Abuse and Neglect Standards* and conferees clearly recommended that lawyers for children should act as lawyers, not as guardians *ad litem.*[49] The co-sponsors and participants at the Fordham conference included national children's law organizations and many ABA entities.[50]

Ten years later in 2006, children's law experts gathered again at a conference at the University of Nevada, Las Vegas (UNLV), to review the state of legal representation of children. Like the Fordham Conference, the UNLV participants produced a set of recommendations.[51] The UNLV Recommendations encourage lawyers to seek to empower children by helping them develop decision-making capacity. Regarding the role of the lawyer, the UNLV Recommendations strongly support client-directed representation for children capable of making considered decisions.[52] Again, the list of co-sponsors and participants included nationally respected children's law organizations and many ABA entities.[53]

Consistent with the *ABA Abuse and Neglect Standards,* ABA policy, and the recommendations of national children's law experts, Section 3 of this Model Act mandates that an attorney, acting in a traditional role, should be appointed for every child who is the subject of an abuse or neglect proceeding.[54] Attorneys can identify legal issues regarding their child clients, use their legal skills to ensure the protection of their clients' rights and needs, and advocate for their clients. The Model Act requires lawyers to complete a thorough and independent investigation and participate fully in all stages of the litigation. Lawyers for children, as lawyers for any client, have a role as a counselor to their clients and should assist their clients in exploring the practical effects of taking various positions, the likelihood that a court will accept particular arguments, and the impact of such decisions on the child, other family members, and future legal proceedings.[55]

Lawyers for children allow children to be participants in the proceedings that affect their lives and safety. Children who are represented by a lawyer often feel the process is fairer because they had a chance to participate and to be heard. Consequently, children are more likely to accept the court's decision because of their own involvement in the process.

Requiring lawyers to represent children in abuse and neglect cases is also consistent with federal law. The Child Abuse Prevention and Treatment Act (CAPTA) requires the appointment of a "guardian *ad litem*" for a child as a condition of receiving federal funds for child abuse prevention and treatment programs. Providing a child with a lawyer is consistent with the requirements of CAPTA. No state with a lawyer model has been held out of compliance with CAPTA and Health and Human Services (HHS) has issued guidance suggesting that appointing counsel for a child promotes the child's "best interest" consistent with CAPTA.[56]

The Model Act also provides lawyers guidance when representing children with diminished capacity, which includes young children. Like all children in these proceedings, young children are entitled to proceedings that fully examine and address their needs, including *inter alia* their physical, behavioral, and developmental health and well-being, their education and early-learning needs, their need for family permanency and stability, and their need to be safe from harm. The Model Act also allows states to set an age of capacity if they so choose.

The Model Act allows and welcomes "best interest advocates" in child welfare cases. A best interest advocate is defined as "an individual, not functioning or intended to function as the child's lawyer, appointed by the court to assist in determining the best interests of the child."[57] The advisor may be a court-appointed special advocate (CASA), a guardian *ad litem* or other person who has received training specific to the best interest of the child. The Act endorses and in no way restricts the widespread use of CASAs to fulfill the role of court appointed advisor.[58]

A state's law regarding abuse and neglect proceedings should be designed to provide children involved in an abuse and neglect case with a well-trained, high quality lawyer who is well-compensated and whose caseload allows for effective representation. Lawyers for children are essential for ensuring that the child's legal rights are protected. "Unless children are allowed by lawyers to set the objectives of their cases, they would not only be effectively deprived of a number of constitutional rights, they would be denied procedures that are fundamental to the rule of law."[59]

Children in dependency court proceedings are often taken from their parents, their siblings and extended families, their schools, and everything that is familiar to them. Children and youth deserve a voice when important and life-altering decisions are being made about them. They deserve to have their opinions heard, valued and considered. They have interests that are often distinct or are opposed to those of the state and their parents in dependency proceedings and, as the ABA has recognized many times, they deserve ethical legal representation.

In preparing this Model Act, the drafters have taken into consideration the enormous contributions of various organizations and advocates in defining standards of representation, most notably that of the American Bar Association (ABA), the National Association of Counsel for Children (NACC), the Uniform Law Commission (ULC), participants in the Representing Children in Families UNLV Conference, and the states themselves. In addition, drafters have sought input from the ABA Standing Committee on Ethics, various sections within the ABA, and more than 30 children's law centers around the country who represent children every day.

Respectfully Submitted,
Hilarie Bass, Chair
Section of Litigation
August, 2011

NOTES

1. This Model Act was drafted as a collaboration between the ABA Section of Litigation Children's Rights Litigation Committee, the Bar-Youth Empowerment Program of the ABA Center on Children and the Law, and First Star. The Act incorporates some language from the provisions of the NCCUSL Representation of Children in Abuse, Neglect, and Custody Proceedings Act.

2. NCCUSL, 2006 *Uniform Representation of Children in Abuse, Neglect, and Custody Proceedings*, Sec. 2(2) [Hereinafter NCCUSL Act]

3. *Id.*, Sec. 2(6); American Bar Association *Standards of Practice for Lawyers Who Represent Children in Abuse and Neglect Cases*, Part I, Sec A-1, *Family Law Quarterly* 29, 1995, 375. The standards were formally adopted by the ABA House of Delegates in 1996. [Hereinafter ABA Standards].

4. ABA Standards, Part I, Sec A-3.

5. NCCUSL Act, Sec. 4(c); *see also* ABA Standards, Part I, Sec B-1.

6. ABA Standards, Sec D-13; F-1-5; *see generally* La. Sup. Ct. R. XXXIII, Standard 1; *see generally* Ariz. R. Proc. Juv. Ct. R. 39(b).

7. ABA Standards, Part II, Sec L-1-2.

8. NCCUSL Act, Sec. 9

9. *Id.*, Sec. 10(a)

10. ABA Standards, Part I, Sec D-13; F-1-5; *see generally* La. Sup. Ct. R. XXXIII, Standard 1.; *see generally* Ariz. R. Proc. Juv. Ct. R. 39(b).

11. NCCUSL Act, Sec. 11 Alternative A.

12. ABA Standards, Part I, Section D-12.

13. *Id.*

14. ABA Model Rules of Professional Responsibility (hereinafter M.R.) 1.2

15. M.R. 1.6

16. M.R. 1.3

17. M.R. 1.1

18. M.R. 1.7

19. M.R. 1.4

20. M.R. 2.1

21. ABA Standards, commentary A-1

22. M.R. 1.4

23. M.R. 2.1

24. Massachusetts Committee for Public Counsel Services. *Performance Standards Governing the Representation Of Children And Parents in Child Welfare Cases*, Chapter Four: Performance Standards and Complaint Procedures 4-1, Section 1.6(c) (2004).

25. Candice L. Maze, JD. *Advocating for Very Young Children in Dependency Proceedings: The Hallmarks of Effective, Ethical Representation.* Washington, DC: ABA Center on Children and the Law, October, 2010.

26. *Id.*

27. *Id.*

28. *Id.*

29. M.R. 1.14(c)

30. Restatement (Third) of the Law Governing Lawyers Sec. 24 c. c (2000).

31. M.R. 1.14 cmt. 1

32. M.R. 1.14, cmt. 1

33. Anne Graffam Walker, Ph.D. *Handbook on Questioning Children: A Linguistic Perspective* 2nd Edition. Washington, DC: ABA Center on Children and the Law, 1999.

34. M.R. 1.14 cmt. 5

35. M.R. 1.14 cmt. 5

36. M.R. 1.14, cmt. 8

37. M.R. 1.14, cmt. 8

38. M.R. 1.14, cmt 8

39. NCCUSL Act, Sec. 15

40. NCCUSL Act, Sec. 16

41. American Bar Association Youth Transitioning from Foster Care August 2007; American Bar Association Foster Care Reform Act August 2005

42. N.C. Gen. Stat. Ann. § 7B-603.

43. NCCUSL Act, Sec. 19.

44. Kenny A. v. Perdue, 356 F. Supp. 2d 1353 (2005).

45. American Bar Association, *ABA Standards of Practice for Lawyers Who Represent Children in Abuse and Neglect Cases* (1996) at preface.

46. American Bar Association, *ABA Standards of Practice for Lawyers Who Represent Children in Abuse and Neglect Cases* (1996) The Standards can be found at *http://www.abanet. org/leadership/2006/annual/onehundredfourteen.doc*

47. *Uniform Representation of Children in Abuse and Neglect, and Custody Proceedings Act* (hereinafter "NCCUSL Act"), National Conference of Commissioners of Uniform State Law. Prefatory Note (2007); the text of the final act can be found at *http://www. law.upenn.edu/bll/archives/ulc/rarccda/2007_final.htm. See* Atwood, *supra* note 1, at 188-91; Davidson, Howard A. "Child Protection Policy and Practice at Century's End." *Family Law Quarterly* 33, 1999, 765, 768-69. For information about different state practices *see Representing Children Worldwide*, 2005 (*www.law.yale.edu/rcw*) or *A Child's Right to Counsel. First Star's National Report Card on Legal Representation for Children*, 2007.

48. ABA Model Act, Commentary to Section 7(c) which refers to ABA Model Rules 1.2, 1.6, 1.3, 1.1, 1.7, 1.4 and 2.1.

49. "Recommendations of the Conference on Ethical Issues in the Legal Representation of Children," 64 *Fordham Law Review* 64, 1996, 1301 (Fordham Recommendations) (attorney must follow child's expressed preferences and attempt to discern wishes in context in developmentally appropriate way if child is incapable of expressing viewpoint).

50. Co-sponsors included the Administration for Children, Youth and Families, U.S. Department of Health and Human Services; ABA Center on Children and the Law, Young Lawyers Division; ABA Center for Professional Responsibility, ABA Section of Criminal Justice, Juvenile Justice Committee; ABA Section of Family Law; ABA Section of Individual Rights and Responsibilities; ABA Section of Litigation Task Force on Children; ABA Steering Committee on the Unmet Legal Needs of Children; Juvenile Law Center; National Association of Counsel for Children; National Center for Youth Law; National Counsel of Juvenile and Family Court Judges; Stein Center for Ethics and Public Interest Law, Fordham University School of Law.

51. *See* "Recommendations of the UNLV Conference on Representing Children in Families: Children's Advocacy and Justice Ten Years after Fordham." *Nevada Law Journal* 6, 2006, 592-687 (UNLV Recommendations).

52. As stated in the Recommendations, "[c]hildren's attorneys should take their direction from the client and should not substitute for the child's wishes the attorney's own judgment of what is best for children or for that child." *Id.* at 609.

53. Co-sponsors of UNLV included the ABA Center on Children and the Law, Young Lawyers Division; ABA Center for Professional Responsibility; ABA Child Custody and Adoption Pro Bono Project; ABA Section of Family Law; ABA Section of Litigation; Home at Last, Children's Law Center of Los Angeles; Juvenile Law Center; National Association of Counsel for Children; National Center for Youth Law; National Council of Juvenile and Family Court Judges; National Juvenile Defender Center; Stein Center for Law and Ethics, Fordham University School of Law; Support Center for Child Advocates; and Youth Law Center.

54. Federal law has long authorized the discretionary appointment of counsel for Indian children subject to the Indian Child Welfare Act. *See* 25 U.S.C. § 1912(b) (2000).

55. Model Act, Commentary for Section (7)(c)(1).

56. U.S. Department of Health and Human Services, Children's Bureau. *Adoption 2002: The President's Initiative on Adoption and Permanence for Children*, Commentary to Guideline 15A.

57. Model Act, Section 1.

58. The Court Appointed Special Advocate is a lay volunteer who advocates as a nonlawyer on behalf of a child in child abuse and neglect proceedings. Volunteers are screened and trained at the local level, but all CASA programs that are affiliated with the National Court Appointed Special Advocate Association must comply with the standards issued by that organization. *See www.nationalcasa.org.* In addition, many states have established their own standards to ensure that the volunteers representing children are competent and possess relevant training and experience. *See generally* Piraino, Michael S. "Lay Representation of Abused and Neglected Children: Variations on Court Appointed Special Advocate Programs and Their Relationship to Quality Advocacy." *Journal of Center for Children and the Courts* 1, 1999, 63. The Office of Juvenile Justice and Delinquency Prevention of the United States Department of Justice is authorized to enter into cooperative agreements with the National CASA Association to expand CASA programs nationally. *See* 42 U.S.C.A. § 13013 (2005 & Supp. 2006). One of the key strengths of the CASA program is that a CASA volunteer generally represents only one child at a time. Moreover, an attorney for the child working in tandem with a CASA volunteer can provide a powerful "team" approach in juvenile court. In addition, CASA volunteers may have access to the CASA program's own legal representative for legal advice.

59. Guggenheim, Martin. "A Paradigm for Determining the Role of Counsel for Children." *Fordham Law Review* 64, 1996, 1399, 1423-24.

Legal Representation in Child Welfare Proceedings

Benefits of
high-quality legal representation

 Protects parents' and children's legal rights.

 Increases parties' participation in and out of court.

 Improves all parties' perceptions of fairness.

 Reduces delays in achieving permanency and helps children and families reach better, long-term outcomes.

 Promotes tailored case plans and services.

 Improves frequency and timeliness of parent-child and sibling visitation and family time.

 Empowers families and communities to keep children safe at home.

 Informs better judicial decision making.

 Saves jurisdictions money by reducing time children spend in foster care.

Structuring a system of high-quality representation

- ✔ Clearly define roles and expectations.
- ✔ Set reasonable caseloads.
- ✔ Offer fair compensation and benefits.
- ✔ Follow standards of practice.
- ✔ Provide specialized child welfare law training.
- ✔ Ensure effective supervision.
- ✔ Seek client feedback on representation.
- ✔ Give attorneys access to an interdisciplinary model of representation.

How judges promote high-quality legal representation

- ✔ Ensure all parties have access to legal representation as early as possible in the case.
- ✔ Confirm all counsel have requisite training, experience and understanding of child welfare law to vigorously represent their clients.
- ✔ Establish an environment where parties are treated with respect, patience, dignity, courtesy, and as part of the problem-solving process.
- ✔ Understand the child welfare agency's practices, procedures, and operations, and ensure it fulfills its legal duties.
- ✔ Require that all attorneys adopt a disciplined approach to processing cases and respect timely court hearings, court decisions, and implementation of court orders.
- ✔ Ensure the spirit of collaborative meetings and case management does not compromise any party's rights and protections under the law.
- ✔ Seek opportunities to train child welfare attorneys.
- ✔ Solicit input from all parties to gain as complete a picture as possible to inform judicial decision making and promote child and family well-being.

Essential practices for all child welfare attorneys

- ✔ Advocate for your client.
- ✔ Ensure judges have information needed to make case decisions.
- ✔ Communicate with clients regularly.
- ✔ Know federal and state child welfare laws and keep current on new developments.
- ✔ Prepare for and attend court hearings and reviews.
- ✔ Seek court accommodations that promote equal access and full participation in proceedings.
- ✔ Prepare clients and witnesses for court.
- ✔ Maintain a reasonable caseload and devote sufficient time for advocacy.
- ✔ Conduct a thorough, independent investigation at every stage of the case.

- ✔ Provide ethical legal representation.
- ✔ Understand and effectively implement trauma-informed practice.
- ✔ Confirm clients receive proper notice and comply with court orders.
- ✔ Actively engage in conflict resolution and negotiation.
- ✔ Reduce case continuances and timely file all pleadings, motions, and briefs.
- ✔ Mentor and train others in the field.
- ✔ File motions and appeals to protect client rights and interests.
- ✔ Understand how cultural, social, and economic differences affect the attorney-client relationship and avoid personal and system bias.

Quality hallmarks

 Child attorney

 Parent attorney

 Agency attorney

Role: Protect and advance child's interests in court, provide legal counsel, and help the child understand the legal process and feel empowered to participate.

Quality hallmarks:
- Understand the child's wishes in the case.
- Understand the child's strengths, needs, and resources.
- Ensure the child has an opportunity to attend and participate in court hearings.
- Advocate for the child to maintain contact with parents, siblings, and kin through visitation, placement, and permanency planning.
- Work with collateral contacts—teachers, foster parents, service providers.
- Collaborate with a multidisciplinary team.
- Promote tailored, specific case plans and services.
- Advocate for the child's access to education and community supports.

Role: Protect the parent's legal rights, advance the parent's interests in court, and help the parent understand the legal process.

Quality hallmarks:
- Explain the child welfare legal system and the parent's rights and duties.
- Ensure the parent's voice is heard and understood in the proceedings.
- Help the parent problem solve and meet case goals.
- Build a relationship of trust and ensure the parent experiences fairness.
- Understand the parent's life circumstances, including strengths, needs, and available resources.
- Advocate parent-child contact through visitation and permanency planning.
- Collaborate with a multidisciplinary team, including parent mentors and parent social workers.
- Address collateral legal issues that may affect the child welfare case in housing, employment, health care, disabilities, domestic violence, benefits, criminal justice, and immigration law.

Role: Represent the child welfare agency or jurisdiction and present evidence of the underlying case in court including agency compliance with federal and state child welfare laws.

Quality hallmarks:
- Provide guidance to agencies and caseworkers on child welfare law, procedures and policies.
- Consult on decisions to remove or return a child and ensure decisions meet legal standards.
- Prepare or help prepare the initial petition and subsequent pleadings.
- Promote quality casework and agency performance to support families.
- Ensure no undue delays in service provision, case planning, or other agency duties.
- Cooperate and communicate regularly with other counsel.
- Help the agency meet federal monitoring and continuous quality improvement requirements.
- Work with agency to ensure parties' legal rights are protected.
- Train caseworkers on federal and state laws to ensure the agency maintains high-quality performance.